Champions . . . Plus

Blessings!

Mark Strickland

Phil. 4:13

Champions . . . Plus

Gary DeVaul,
Mark Thallander
& Friends

Aventine Press

Champions . . . Plus
Copyright © 2007 by the Mark A. Thallander Trust

Unless otherwise noted, Scripture quotations are taken from the New American Standard Bible®,
Copyright © 1960, 1962, 1963, 1968, 1971, 1972, 1973, 1975, 1977, 1995 by The Lockman Foundation.
Used by permission. (www.Lockman.org)

Scripture quotations marked ESV are from The Holy Bible, English Standard Version®, copyright © 2001 by Crossway Bibles, a publishing ministry of Good News Publishers. Used by permission. All rights reserved.

Scripture quotations marked NIV are taken from the Holy Bible, NEW INTERNATIONAL VERSION®. Copyright © 1973, 1978, 1984 International Bible Society. All rights reserved throughout the world. Used by permission of International Bible Society.

Scripture quotations marked RSV are taken from the Revised Standard Version of the Bible, copyright 1952 [2nd edition, 1971] by the Division of Christian Education of the National Council of Churches of the Churches of Christ in the United States of America. Used by permission. All rights reserved.

Portions of this book were originally published under the title *Champions*, © 2004 by Gary DeVaul, and are reprinted with the permission of Grant D. DeVaul.

Published by Aventine Press
1023 4th Ave. #204
San Diego, CA 92101
www.aventinepress.com

ISBN: 1-59330-501-X

Printed in the United States of America

Champions . . . Plus

is dedicated in loving memory of

the Reverend Gary Allen DeVaul

and

Mae Bernice Branvold Thallander

Champions
by Gary DeVaul
(included in this expanded edition)

was dedicated in loving memory of

Dr. Raymond Beckering

and

Wilfred Lasse Emmanuel Thallander

Contents

Foreword

One will spend all of life journeying.

Bold words for a mere musician, don't you think? "Perhaps," some would say. "Not at all," say others. "I would never get anywhere if that were the case!" I would like for us to take together a trip towards a more profound experience of everyday life. Guiding this adventure will be Mark Thallander, musician, mentor, and friend. Mark is an organist by vocation and a worship leader by calling. His is a story of profound proportions, made ever more real after a tragic accident in 2003. Let us journey with him toward a better understanding of God's hand in our lives and of our feet on God's path.

In the day-to-day of you and me, we will venture towards various ends by various means. When Mark was growing up, the same was also true. He would practice the piano nearly every day. The end: a polished piece of music, simple in its constructs and profound in its pedagogical purpose. The means: practice, practice, practice! In college, there were final exams to take and recitals to be performed. In young adulthood, jobs and a career to establish, relationships to nurture, and marks of financial security to establish. For the life of this church musician, each was a noble quest toward a noble end.

Sunday morning service music is always quite an end indeed, especially with millions of people watching live on television each week! Being an organist at one of the most visible churches in North America was surely more than just a full-time job. It was a calling. The prelude needed to begin at the proper moment to ensure accurate timing of the start of the service. The hymns needed to be prepared and enhanced with key changes, interludes, and uplifting alternate harmonizations, bringing the text to life. Choir rehearsal was essential earlier in the week, anthems memorized, so all could be prepared and not hinder worship by sloppy technical mistakes or uninspiring musical interpretation. Hours and hours Mark spent at the organ console, just for Easter and Christmas alone.

And the end?   A beautiful, Spirit-led, purposeful, and meaningful experience of worship, for each individual participating. Mark frequently speaks of the honor of knowing that God uses people through their unique gifts which have been bestowed upon them. In the mind of the mere human, it is simply too awesome to comprehend. God took our friend Mark, along with every participant in the service, to the goal of each different journey, each Sunday, each holiday, each funeral, and each wedding.

But what of the means? What about the pilgrimage, if you will, toward these noble ends? The studying, preparation, and practicing? May I be so bold as to offer that the journey itself can truly be the noble end? That the process of preparing the hymn is just as spiritually fulfilling as playing it in the service? That choir rehearsal can minister to the choir just as much as it does to the congregation on Sunday? Or what of the pastor preparing the sermon? Time spent in the Word, studying its context, meaning, and contemporary application, speaks volumes to the pastor, well before ever stepping foot into the pulpit.

It's early August 2003, and Mark is within days of celebrating his fifty-third birthday. He is very happy about the exciting adventures he has taken together with God. Over five decades of exhilaration, nervousness, contentment, fear, pleasure, and pain. Many seemingly impossible obstacles were conquered with God in control. Things Mark never dreamt of fell into place just ever so perfectly. The unattainable was gladly provided to him, blessing after blessing, trial after trial. It seemed as if after undergoing so many different journeys with our Lord, that he would have experienced most of them already.

Reflect, if you will, on the evening of August 3, 2003. Mark is returning from Massachusetts to the home of a dear and lifelong friend in Maine. The day is Sunday, dusk is setting in, and he is driving alone. Torrential rain is pouring down, and his speed is reduced on the highway. The destination is not far: a warm meal, a cozy home, and a friend in Maine. The end of the day's short journey from Worcester to Ogunquit. As he exits the turnpike, the vehicle begins to hydroplane out of control, and within seconds Mark is in a ditch at the end of the ramp and at the beginning of the most challenging, obstacle-filled journey one could ever experience.

No challenge that he has ever faced compares to the challenge of this quest, this voyage, this trip toward the unknown: life with only one arm. But what is the end of this adventure? What is the purpose of having an arm ripped away from you? To what objective does one work toward? And by what means does one reach that end?

The answer is clear, excitingly clear! The end is, of course, the journey itself. That is the goal toward which we are all to proceed: the goal of "one step at a time," Jeremiah 29:11, and "though the wrong seems oft so strong, God is the ruler yet."[1]

Spiritual growth is something that we endeavor to experience. God gives us many tools to fuel the fires of maturity. Tools like friends, hymns, church services, quiet moments of serenity, passages of Scripture, time reading what others interpret of that Scripture, and family, just to name a few. Losing an arm and needing to relearn how to eat, wash his hair, change his clothes, play the organ, and conduct a choir with his remaining arm are just some of the new tools our friend Mark has now been blessed with. Each of these was once an easier task, second nature in its execution. Now, each is rebirthed and transformed into a whole new set of tools with which to experience God in new ways.

Relationships are very important to Mark. God has blessed him with so many generous people who have lent their helping hands in every way. Friendships have solidified further now. God has spoken to Mark from each of them, teaching him new insights and lessons in love. Individuals surrounding him are availing themselves to the hands of God, each being a specific and crucial instrument. Many may not even realize how God has spoken to Mark through them and what they do for him. The dawning of this profound gratitude is simply incomprehensible for words.

God's family is vast. Because of this tragedy, people of different denominations have found themselves working side by side, growing closer to each other as they pour out *phileo* love for a wounded brother. Their intimacies with each other deepen as the Lord ministers to them and through them. One should sit back and observe how God works in other people's lives and bask in what has happened in their own. It is a truly awesome sight.

In the wreckage, the future of our friend Mark Thallander was seemingly uncertain. In the hospital, his future was definitely uncertain. With his father hospitalized several thousand miles away, important decisions needed to be made. Mark's livelihood seemed doomed from that point forward. How can one play the organ with only hand? Or direct a choir? How do I earn money in order to eat and pay bills? How do I turn to the next page of music?

In his new life as an amputee, the future is crystal clear. Peace, hope, excitement, and love abound. God wants us all to endeavor forward, always focusing on the goal of being a better adventurer and learning to trust Him more and more. That is the end to which we all journey. Mark's challenges are great. After reading the book of Job in a completely new light, he thought he had found another best friend who could relate to his every difficulty. In his new life, Mark has only one arm. The right arm is gladly working overtime to make up the difference! Losing a father and an arm in the same week would make even the strongest collapse and the proudest weep. Who would have imagined that tragedies such as these could yield such positive results? God is in control. God holds Mark's life and yours in the palm of His hand.

I am glad to report that Mark knows how to wash his hair with one hand. He can play the organ with one hand. After all, he indeed has two fully functional feet! He can even direct a choir *and* turn the page with only one hand. God has helped him learn. God has helped us all learn. Together, we are using the new tools that God has given to Mark for spiritual enrichment. What will be next? How will God touch the life of one we may not even know through these experiences? It's exciting to see what God can do, isn't it?

In these next chapters, join our friend in his journey. Travel for a bit, stay as long as you like, return to visit often. Mark's prayer is that his story will be used by the Lord to encourage you, to bring you joy and hope, and to affect you profoundly. See how God can use even a one-armed organist to minister to the flock. Come and taste this road now traveled, where our footsteps are indeed the destination, and where "though the wrong seems oft so strong, God is the ruler yet!"[2]

Jeremy McElroy

1. "This Is My Father's World" by Maltbie D. Babcock.
2. See note 1 above.

Preface
to
Champions . . . Plus

Since *Champions* was first published in 2004, Gary DeVaul, its author, and I heard from countless numbers of people how they were blessed by this collection of devotional writings about my accident and the initial months along the road to recovery. But rather than reprinting it, my brother, Wayne, suggested that the book be expanded to include more information about what happened in the months and years following the accident. Gary, a very creative mind and a magnificent writer, invited me to join him for a new book project. We would share in the writing, expressing our thoughts on the same subject from our own unique and personal perspectives.

I was in Ogunquit, Maine, in January 2006. At that time, Gary outlined the table of contents and wrote an introduction to our new book. In the summer of 2006 we would plan to be together in Ogunquit and write a chapter each day. Little did we know that one month later, on Sunday, February 26, 2006, Gary would leave us. Held in the loving arms of his youngest son, Phil, Gary was transferred into the everlasting arms of Jesus.

Our annual Choral Festival was that evening. Gary was in the Los Angeles area for the Festival and was scheduled to offer the opening prayer. Many people were looking forward to meeting him. In fact, Gary was to have had an autograph party in the gift shop of the Cathedral of Our Lady of the Angels before the concert began. Instead, Lois Bock made the shocking announcement at the beginning of the Festival about Gary's death and that we would be dedicating the evening in memory of Gary, one of our dear friends and Advisory Council members.

With the written contributions of many friends, I have been able to compile this book which gives both information about and inspiration from what happened since my accident in August 2003 until 2006. I want to especially thank Larry and Marcy Smith, Paul Pare, and Michael Ferry who graciously opened their homes in Ogunquit, so I could write in the "beautiful place by the sea" where so much of the story happened, and I would also like to thank the Ogunquit Baptist Church for allowing me daily rehearsal time on the pipe organ. To my brother, Wayne, and Aunt Delores "Dodie" Smith who encouraged me as I worked on this book in Stockton, California (Aunt Dodie also kept me sustained with delicious meals morning, noon, and night) – I am indeed grateful! And special thanks to long-time friend from Garden Grove Community Church years, Jan Rodger, who carefully edited both *Champions* and *Champions . . . Plus.*

I know Gary would want me to thank all of you who prayed for him. He appreciated your cards and calls so very much. I especially remember Gary as I write this, as today is his birthday. It is with a grateful heart that I also thank you for your many prayers on my behalf and for all the support and encouragement you have given me. Once again, I say to all of you, God loves you and so do I!

Mark A. Thallander
Palm Springs, California
June 29, 2007

Preface
to
Champions

It was January 1976. I began my first full-time music ministry position at Garden Grove Community Church in Southern California. There I met a dynamic youth minister and, wonder of wonders, he loved the organ! Each month his college group would have a potluck dinner on the church campus, followed by a Communion service in the Chapel-in-the-Sky. There I would play for that special group in that unique setting.

That was my entrance to a lifelong friendship with Gary DeVaul and his family. I would occasionally "babysit" his three sons – Grant, Matt, and Phil – and experienced many wonderful social occasions in their Villa Park home. Especially memorable were the annual Christmas gatherings with magnificent carol singing and the times when Marcia would invite me over for dinner – my favorite – "beef-in-a-bag"!

The boys, now all graduated from college, lead a bicoastal existence. Some years ago Gary moved to the East Coast. He invited me to visit him in the quaint resort village of Ogunquit, Maine. After several years of coaxing, I finally accepted his invitation – and absolutely loved it! I've returned annually, each summer extending my visit for as long as possible. And, once again, I've had opportunity to enjoy "beef-in-a-bag"!

It was August 3, 2003. I played the organ in Worcester, Massachusetts. A summer storm followed me from Massachusetts, through New Hampshire and into Maine. Dinner was in the oven. Gary was waiting . . . but I never arrived. The car hydroplaned at the exit from the turnpike, just minutes from my destination.

I experienced the deafening silence after the explosion of the accident. There were coins, shoes, clothes, boxes of CDs, and videotapes flying through the interior of the car. My glasses and cell phone were thrust to the floor. There was a woman's voice speaking to me, giving me encouragement and instruction. There were the sights and sounds of sirens, and firefighters and paramedics breaking windows and trying to determine how best to retrieve me from the wreckage. The ambulance ride forty miles to Portland, Maine. The surgeons having me sign an amputation release form. Me pleading with them to save my arm . . . and to call Gary DeVaul.

To save my life, the surgeons quickly rushed me into surgery. I had lost over half of my blood. Gary arrived following the surgery. And he was there for me every day . . . in the hospital . . . when I received the call from my brother informing me of my father's death seven days after my accident . . . in the rehabilitation center . . . and during my outpatient rehab in York, Maine. How fitting that Gary's carefully crafted and spiritually sensitive writings of that experience are now in book form. I trust this book will be enriching to you, the reader, and to hundreds of others across this nation and around the world!

Thank you, Gary, for your many years of friendship. Your care and support have gone way beyond the call of duty. You became the hands of Christ to me, and I am forever grateful. God loves you and do I!

Mark A. Thallander
Pasadena, California
March 2004

Contributors

Greg Asimakoupoulos – author, pastor, Mercer Island, Washington.

Paul Bandy – grant writer; chair, Mark A. Thallander Trust; administrator, member, Board of Directors, Mark Thallander Foundation, Pasadena, California.

Jacque I. Blauvelt – registered nurse, licensed minister, Springfield, Missouri.

Lois Bock – freelance writer; speaker; chairman of the board, Fred Bock Music Companies, Tarzana, California; member, Board of Directors, Mark Thallander Foundation.

David Clark – former pastor, Ogunquit Baptist Church, Ogunquit, Maine; pastor, Court Street Baptist Church, Auburn, Maine.

Leanne Cusimano – owner, Amore Breakfast, Ogunquit, Maine; member, Advisory Council, Mark Thallander Foundation.

Pamela Decker – composer, organist, professor of organ/music theory, University of Arizona, Tucson.

Ross Dixon – worship coordinator and organist, St. Paul's Presbyterian Church, Ottawa, Canada; member, Advisory Council, Mark Thallander Foundation.

Diane Geisler – Mark Thallander's cousin, Vacaville, California.

Judith Hanlon – pastor, Hadwen Park Congregational Church, UCC, Worcester, Massachusetts.

Rosemary Jackson – special assistant to the president for alumni relations, Vanguard University, Costa Mesa, California; member, Advisory Council, Mark Thallander Foundation.

John W. Kennedy – associate editor, *Today's Pentecostal Evangel,* Springfield, Missouri.

Eric Dale Knapp – conductor-in-residence, Carnegie Hall, New York City; music director and member, Board of Directors, Mark Thallander Foundation.

Jeremy McElroy – commercial pilot, organist/pianist, Atlanta, Georgia; member, Board of Directors, Mark Thallander Foundation; Mark's duet partner.

Stephen McWhorter – founder and rector emeritus, St. David's Episcopal Church, Ashburn, Virginia.

Joyce Pryor – Mark Thallander's cousin, Pittsburg, California.

Jan Rodger – eDOT curriculum coordinator and editor, Greater Europe Mission, Monument, Colorado.

Steve Scauzillo – editorial page editor, San Gabriel Valley Newspaper Group, San Gabriel, California.

Alicia Steinhaus – graphic designer; director, Lake Avenue Youth Orchestra, Pasadena, California; member, Board of Directors, Mark Thallander Foundation.

Frederick Swann – organist emeritus, Crystal Cathedral, Garden Grove, California; national president, American Guild of Organists; member, Board of Directors, Mark Thallander Foundation.

John West – organist, former artist-in-residence, Bel Air Presbyterian Church, Los Angeles, California; member, Advisory Council, Mark Thallander Foundation.

Photographic Contributors

Front cover photo of Mark Thallander at the piano by John Isenberg
Back cover photo of Mark Thallander by Christopher Smith
Back cover photo of Gary DeVaul by Alicia Steinhaus

Interior photos courtesy of David and Wandah Clark, Leanne Cusimano, John Isenberg, Angie Johnson, Thelma Kok, Jeremy McElroy, Carlo Nittoli, Joyce Pryor, Jan Rodger, Alicia Steinhaus, Wayne Thallander, and the Mark Thallander Trust and Foundation.

All photos are reproduced by permission.

In the Beginning

by Mark Thallander

It was January 2003. I had arrived in London with a small group of choir directors and organists. We were in the British Isles, preparing to tour the great cathedrals and churches of England, Scotland, and Ireland. And to hear as many historic pipe organs as possible! While there, I learned that, back in Stockton, California, my father was in the hospital where he had been diagnosed with diabetes and my mother had suffered a series of mini-strokes. My brother, Wayne, and my Aunt Dodie and Uncle Glen were taking turns caring for them. I called to talk with them as often as possible.

After returning to the U.S., I felt I should go to Stockton and care for Mom and Dad on a full-time basis. I requested to be excused from my contract as an adjunct professor of music at Glendale College for the spring semester. Additionally, I had just been offered the parish organist position at the Church of Our Saviour in San Gabriel, just minutes from where I lived in Pasadena. My friends in Southern California were very supportive, so off to Northern California I went. I was very familiar with the Stockton area, having lived there from first grade through high school.

Since my father now needed a sodium-free and sugar-free diet, I began attending free classes at Saint Joseph's Medical Center to learn what to cook for him. I took Mom and Dad to their numerous doctor and rehabilitation appointments, grocery shopping, banking, and to church – and helped them with laundry and cleaning the house. Wayne and Dodie took care of the medications, keeping the morning and evening pill boxes appropriately filled. My job was simply to make sure that my parents took their pills. Dad, at age 91, who had loved and eaten ice cream, cake, cookies, and candy all of his life, was now checking his blood sugar level many times daily. He was amazing in his dedication to only eat and drink what was on his new diet.

Long-time neighbors, friends, and relatives stopped by to see Mom and Dad on a regular basis. Next-door neighbor Jim, who had worked with my father, often came to visit two or three times a day. Cousins Diane and Joyce and Aunt Eva stayed one weekend when I was scheduled to be the substitute organist at Grace Community Church in Southern California. While in Stockton, I tried to practice the organ as much as possible at Central United Methodist Church and also played at various churches in the area.

Wayne found Mom and Dad a cozy two-bedroom apartment at a spacious retirement complex close to our Aunt Dodie. The Thursday before Palm Sunday, they moved from the home which Mom had helped design in 1965. Since my parents were very well cared for at Rio Las Palmas, I was able to fulfill a previous commitment to play the organ that Sunday morning for the Triumphal Entry celebration at Peninsula Christian Center in Redwood City. After returning to Stockton to make sure that Mom and Dad were adjusting well to their new surroundings, I flew to Springfield, Missouri, where I had been invited to be the guest organist for Good Friday Communion services and Resurrection celebrations at Central Assembly of God.

Even Gary DeVaul, with dog Casey, stopped in Stockton on his return trip to Ogunquit, Maine, after spending time with friends and relatives in California. I never had the nerve to tell Mom that Casey spent the night in their house (I was still staying in the house as it had not yet sold).

Being with Mom and Dad for those five months in 2003 was a tremendous experience for which I will always be grateful. My parents had given so much to me throughout my entire life that it was such an honor and privilege to be able to serve them.

The Summer of 2003

by Mark Thallander

The Vanguard University Concert Choir, which I accompanied, sang at Carnegie Hall and St. Patrick's Cathedral, New York City, in May 2002. Because of those performances, I was invited to return to both venues in June 2003. Associate Organist Stanley Cox invited Jeremy McElroy, my duet partner, and me to present a program on St. Patrick's Cathedral's mammoth pipe organ, and Eric Dale Knapp, conductor-in-residence at Carnegie Hall, arranged for me to play the organ at Carnegie Hall for Beethoven's *Mass in C* and Haydn's *Te Deum*.

Prior to our performance at St. Patrick's, Jeremy and I had played the same duet program in Los Angeles at Cathedral of Our Lady of the Angels. After finishing our bicoastal organ recitals, we traveled to the Ogunquit (Maine) Baptist Church where we added Bach's Concerto in C Minor for Two Pianos to our program. We loved playing for services and concerts at the Ogunquit church where we had become friends with so many people. These annual summer musical events were a dream of Pastor David and Wandah Clark as outreaches to this resort village community . . . and Jeremy and I happily shared our ministry of music with the standing-room-only, enthusiastic crowds!

*Mark Thallander and Jeremy McElroy pose at the organ console after their June
2003 recital at the Cathedral of Our Lady of the Angels in Los Angeles.*

I then flew to Ottawa, Ontario, Canada, where Ross and
Heather Dixon hosted me (spoiled me!), and I participated in a
concert at their church, St. Paul's Presbyterian Church, where Ross
is worship coordinator and organist. Also in Ottawa, I presented a
lecture, "The Use of Organ in Blended Worship: What's in YOUR
Blender?" at the National Library Auditorium for the national
convention of the Royal Canadian College of Organists.

My cousin Karen and her husband had invited me to play for
their daughter's wedding at College Church in Wheaton, Illinois.
Little did I realize, when playing for Jodi and Scott's beautiful
marriage service, it would be the last wedding I would play with both
hands. Karen's mother, my Aunt Dodie, who normally requested
that I play softer, gave me explicit instruction and permission to
"pull out all the stops" for the Widor Toccata recessional! And so
the mighty College Church pipe organ sang with overflowing joy!

(And I was even invited to play an organ solo at church the next morning!) The festive reception concluded by sending Jodi and Scott to Australia for three years of seminary studies. My parents so wanted to be at this wedding but, because of health issues, were unable to make the trip. Instead, they were back in Stockton, California, eagerly waiting to see and hear the promised video.

I flew from Chicago to Washington, D.C., where I had been selected as the organist for the fiftieth anniversary reenactment of the *Revivaltime* radio broadcast in conjunction with the General Council of the Assemblies of God. I had played for this radio ministry, broadcast live every Sunday evening on the ABC radio network, when I was a student at Central Bible College (CBC) and Evangel University in Springfield, Missouri. Beamed across the nation and around the world, *Revivaltime* was heard by millions of listeners on over 700 stations. It had been my dream in high school to play for this weekly broadcast service, and God had given me the desire of my heart. It was an amazing reunion to reconnect with so many choir alumni.

And it was at CBC that I had met Judy Hanlon, now pastoring a New England Congregational church in Worcester, Massachusetts. She had received the new CBC alumni directory, found my e-mail address, and contacted me. Pastor Judy asked if I would consider playing the organ in Worcester on August 3 for a special summer service of worship and Holy Communion.

After saying last-minute good-byes to the many college friends I had seen in Washington, D.C., I flew to Boston. Long-time friend and former co-worker Gary DeVaul picked me up at the airport, and we were off to Gary's place in Ogunquit, Maine. A few days later, Gary loaned me his Toyota 4Runner for my excursion to Worcester – a weekend adventure that would change my life forever!

August 3, 2003

by Mark Thallander

Four churches combined for a special summer Sunday morning service of worship and Holy Communion. Pastor Judy Hanlon eloquently preached as the guest minister in the pulpit of the First Congregational Church in Worcester, Massachusetts. Carefully crafted by Pastor Judy, the service was a meaningful celebration for those who filled the New England-style meeting house. Of course, I didn't know that it would be my last time to play the beloved Widor Toccata as a postlude. Nor did I know that just hours later I would be experiencing a life-threatening situation. Once again I gave the piece my all! And I left the service strengthened by God's presence for the journey ahead.

Pastor Judy invited quite a group of her Hadwen Park congregation to a potluck luncheon at her home following the service. Both of our birthdays were the next week. Just before I left, one of Judy's parishioners, Daniel, gave me a much-needed haircut. Leaving Judy's home for my trip back to Maine, I noticed a large church complex near the highway. It was the First Assembly of God, so I decided to see if Dawn Crabtree, the minister of music, was there. I met Dawn when she attended a performance of *The Glory of Easter* at the Crystal Cathedral. I was informed that she and her husband, David, the senior pastor, were still at the General Council of the Assemblies of God in Washington, D.C., so I left a quick note for her on the organ. I was unaware that a storm was soon to arrive in the New England states. Later I learned that while my friend Tom Matrone was conducting a 1,000-voice youth choir and orchestra at the concluding outdoor prayer service of the General Council on the Capital Mall, the authorities cancelled the rest of the meeting due to the storm. The rain sent the many thousands in attendance scurrying for cover!

The gentle summer's rain became violent as I traveled in the slow lane of the turnpike. In New Hampshire I stopped to get gas. The change was $1.50, which I put on the passenger seat. Nearing Ogunquit, it became increasingly difficult to see, and I missed the York-Ogunquit exit. Instead I would exit at Wells, eleven miles north. Stopping to pay at the toll booth between the two exits, I didn't even need to get my wallet out as the toll was exactly what I had at my fingertips – $1.50. I continued carefully on my journey.

Wow!

by Gary DeVaul

Dinner was sitting too long. Roast chicken and cranberry dressing made with real wild Maine cranberries were waiting. Where is that guy? He can be late, but this is really late. He must be yapping on the phone. But still, the car is under him, pushing him through the black, rainy night.

And then it came. The inevitable phone call. It was our mutual friend Ron. "The State Troopers are trying to get a hold of you, Gary. Your number is unlisted, and they need to talk to you. Mark has had an accident, and with this new privacy thing, they won't give me any information. Stay put. I'm on my way."

But before Ron could arrive, the phone rang again. It was the emergency room. "We need you here, Mr. DeVaul. Mr. Thallander has some serious issues, and he won't let us proceed without you." No details, not a hint. I never would have guessed the truth of the tragedy because the truth, as you know, was unbelievable!

When Mark and I were working at our first full-time positions in ministry at Garden Grove Community Church in the mid-1970s, my venerable friend and mentor was Dr. Raymond Beckering. Ray had a saying for times like these: "Though the wrong seems oft so strong, God is the ruler yet."[1] This line, from the hymn "This Is My Father's World," is rooted in the Calvinist idea of God's sovereignty. And it brings with it a raft of truth. The biblical basis for it can be found in the text of Romans 8:28: "And we know that God causes all things to work together for good to those who love God, to those who are called according to His purpose." Well, that sounds good, but now, pardon the pun, the rubber meets the road.

When Ron and I arrived at the hospital, we were ensconced in a small waiting room off the surgery and recovery areas. The plastic surgeon met us immediately. "We tried to contact you, Gary. Mark wanted us to wait and consult with you before we operated. But the four of us surgeons decided that if we waited, he would bleed to death. He lost over five units of blood. You see, his left arm was severed in three places. The worst of these wounds was at the shoulder of his arm. The impact and seat belt somehow pulled the arm off, tearing the blood vessels and shredding the nerves in such a fashion that it was impossible for us to save the arm. We had to amputate. We thought hard about this, Gary. We know Mark just played concerts at Carnegie Hall and St. Patrick's Cathedral in New York. But we really had no choice. He's conscious now, and he may know what we had to do. But you might find it necessary to tell him."

The Critical Care Unit was dark and gray. There was one other patient to my left as I entered, and then there was my dearest friend, battered and damaged. He was lying on a gurney, a pale light shining on him at the far end of the room. This is not about me, but I have to tell you, crossing that room and getting to his side was like one of those nightmares where you walk in slow motion, struggling against an unseen dread. And yet you make it, and we all know why, don't we?

Mark's eyes opened in little slits. Heavily sedated, still in great pain, he uttered, "Oh, Gary, I'm so glad you're here." In a reflex reaction to the horror of it all, I bent down putting my cheek next to his and saw blood in his ear and on his neck. The nurse came over to his side and whispered to me, "Does he know?" Mark interrupted her. "I remember what the doctor said. Is it true?" I replied, "Yes, it is." Mark sighed, "Oh, wow," closed his eyes, and went to sleep. The nurse told me to get some rest, that I would need it.

Early the next morning Mark and I were visited by the orthopedic surgeon who was part of the decision-making and operating process the night before. Now one of the greatest and most overlooked gifts of God is the gift of humor. All who know Mark are acquainted with his irresistible, dusty, dry wit. That wit, when combined with the power of the Spirit, is awesome and capable of lifting him and everyone else beyond the fog of drugs and pain. A place not fraught with denial, but rather grounded in the words "Though the wrong seems oft so strong . . ."

The doctor wanted to explain to Mark why they had to take his arm. After a rather blunt description, the doctor added, "Now if you want, we have a full complement of pictures of your arm that might help you deal with the situation and understand more fully why we had to amputate." Mark looked at the doctor and, without hesitation, responded, "Do you suppose the pictures would be something I could use in my Christmas letter?" The doctor was stunned! He looked at Mark and said, "Well, we obviously didn't take your sense of humor. That's good, that's healthy." Mark quipped, "No, you didn't, and I won't let you have it either." The moment was instantly transformed! The power of God's Spirit, coupled with Mark's wit, won the day. Mark's sense of humor would continue to make every moment after that an adventure in the Spirit rather than a gruesome tragedy.

Oh yes, there have been profound moments of grief. I was there and we cried together, but there was never a hint of despondency, never hopelessness. One night late, when things had calmed down in the hospital, Mark said to me, as if to encourage me and comfort me, "What a mess, Gary. I'm an organist, a pianist. I just played a concert at St. Patrick's, and I've lost my left arm! This is unbelievable!" And then, moving his right arm through the air from left to right, he continued, "And yet, look at the flowers, and cards, and the Web site. Can you imagine the prayers? I had no idea people could care so much. Think of the things I can do! I can teach, and arrange, and I know I can still play. There are lots of people who will help me."

The next day proved difficult. Mark was given a pump with which to administer himself much-needed morphine. The morphine built up in his system and affected him differently than it would some. They tell me these are called "complications." I thought he was sleeping, though I must admit that I didn't like the sound of his breathing. About that time a good friend, who is a gifted nurse at Massachusetts General Hospital, came into the room to visit. It took only a moment for Paul to hear the sounds of death. He called to Mark. Gently, but purposefully, he slapped Mark's face. Then he lifted Mark's eyelid. Immediately he hit the speaker alarm on the wall and shouted with great authority, "317 STAT!" The room instantly filled with nurses and doctors. Mark was shutting down. His lungs were filling, and he was unconscious. It was an awful moment. They administered the proper medicines and machines of all sorts, and in forty-five minutes Mark was back.

A little later, under the protective care of our very own "St. Paul the nurse," Mark said something that further revealed the spirit we love. Mark called Paul over to his bedside, reached out, and took his hand. "Thanks, Paul, you gave me a hand, and as you can see, I need one. Boy, all the prayers are working, aren't they?" Then Mark gave a little laugh and went back to sleep.

Indeed, Mark, prayers are working, for the power of the Holy Spirit will inspire your friends to lift and love you with their words and deeds. They will use their various gifts as He has used yours. He has used your sense of humor, your personal integrity, your unbridled imagination and creative powers. He will use our gifts as well. Composers will write music for you to play. Universities will hire you to teach. Arrangers will arrange for one hand and two feet. Concerts will be booked. And very importantly, those who can will give hundreds, and yes thousands, for your support. For as our friend Ray Beckering said, "Though the wrong seems oft so strong, God is the ruler yet."

Now as Mark's friend of almost thirty years, I want to say something to you all. Mark and I come out of the great positive tradition of the workplace where we first met. It is a place that teaches and believes in the possibilities of all people when they open themselves to the power of God. The verse "And we know that God causes all things to work together for good to those who love God, to those who are called according to His purpose" is often misused, more often misunderstood. We often hear only the first words of Romans 8:28, "And we know that God causes all things to work together for good," and miss the rest of the passage, "to those who love God, to those who are called according to His purpose." *His* purpose is very simply our faith. If we want to be a part of God's purpose, we must keep the faith as we know it and believe it. My Toyota 4Runner lost its grip, hydroplaned out of control, and look what we have. But WE will not hydroplane. This is where the rubber meets the road for all of us who know and love Jesus Christ.

We must be the ones to sing the chorus for Mark, "That though the wrong seems oft so strong, God is the ruler yet." Then we will turn "Wow!" into wonderful!

1. "This Is My Father's World" by Maltbie D. Babcock.

The Boy with Big Dreams

by Joyce Pryor

Having parents who came from large families provided me with more cousins than I could easily count. The cousins I spent the most time with were Karen and Mark. We would play office, school, and *Revivaltime* broadcast.

When we played office, we had the toy phone and important-looking papers, and we took our jobs very seriously. When we played school, I never got to be the teacher since these two cousins were older. The thing we played most often was *Revivaltime* broadcast. There was an old, upright piano in my room, ready for Mark's favorite activity. We had a small reel-to-reel tape recorder. Mark would play "All Hail the Power of Jesus' Name" and then announce, "Across the nation and around the world, it's *Revivaltime*." We had to get everything just right for Mark, so that meant doing things over if they weren't up to his high expectations. Sometimes we did this "broadcast" for other family members, but the thing I remember most is that we did it a lot! Mark, Karen, and I talked about becoming teachers when we got older, but Mark's biggest dream was to be the pianist for *Revivaltime*. (I also think he wanted his picture on a record album cover!)

In the fall of 1968 and through 1970 Mark attended Central Bible College (CBC) in Springfield, Missouri, and was the pianist for *Revivaltime*. Mark loved touring with the Revivaltime Choir, Choir Director Cyril McLellan, and Radio Evangelist C.M. Ward. He would tell us funny stories about dorm life at CBC and his friends. Mark loved Christian colleges so much that he tried almost all of them. He went to Central, Evangel, Simpson, and Vanguard (where he also served as assistant professor of music from 1998-

2002). Later he earned his Master of Arts in music from California State University, Long Beach (CSULB), and pursued doctoral work in sacred music at the University of Southern California (USC). And yes, he did get on the cover of a few albums!

Mark branched out from piano music to organ music when he had the opportunity to fill in for a vacationing organist, Pat Monk, at his home church, Lincoln Neighborhood Church, in Stockton, California. She taught him quickly to play the organ, and he really liked it. Later he took organ lessons at Simpson, Vanguard, CSULB, and USC. Mark became driven to play church organs as much as possible. It was not uncommon to be on vacation with Mark and he would want to visit the largest churches and ask if he could play their pipe organ. Most of the time he was allowed to play it, so we just had to sit down for a mini-concert!

Pat Monk gave Mark his first organ lessons when he was in high school (a few years before this photo was taken!).

Playing for the *Revivaltime* radio broadcasts had prepared Mark for his participation in the *Hour of Power* telecasts. Mark was elated to play the organ at the Crystal Cathedral in Garden Grove, California, where he served on staff for eighteen years. I really believe some of that "mountain-moving" faith started penetrating Mark's heart through that experience. Mark played at Carnegie Hall and kept being driven to continue in music ministry. He took time off from his busy schedule in the spring of 2003 to help his parents sell their Stockton home and transition into a retirement community. With care and detail, he helped decorate their new home to make it familiar and welcoming for them.

Mark planned to finish his musical commitments in the summer of 2003 and then arrive in Stockton to spend his birthday and his brother's birthday with family. After participating in the *Revivaltime* reenactment at the General Council of the Assemblies of God in Washington, D.C., Mark played on Sunday morning, August 3, in Worcester, Massachusetts, for a pastor he had known at CBC. A summer thunderstorm followed him from Worcester through New Hampshire and into Maine on his return to Gary DeVaul's house. When Mark exited the turnpike, the vehicle he was driving hydroplaned and was thrown into a ditch and then into the oncoming traffic entering the turnpike. Partially hanging by his seatbelt, Mark tried to support himself with his right arm against the passenger door. His seatbelt had shredded his left arm, ripping it from his shoulder. Mark lost over half of his blood. When my sister, Diane, called me with the news, she told me to sit down to hear about Mark losing his left arm. I thought, "Oh no! Music is Mark's whole life; what will he do, now?"

The other news was that Mark's dad (our Uncle Lasse) fell and broke his hip on August 3, the same night as Mark's accident. Mark's brother, Wayne, had to tell his mother about Mark's accident and amputation while Wayne also dealt with hip surgery for their 91-year-old father. They chose not to tell Uncle Lasse about Mark losing his arm. He would take it too hard, and it could interfere with his recovery. Uncle Lasse had hip surgery on Tuesday, August

6. However, he did not recover and passed away on Sunday, August 10. In the meantime, Mark lay in a hospital bed in Portland, Maine, waiting to be released to a rehabilitation center for therapy. During this time of recovery and rehabilitation Mark communicated with us and others on a hospital computer and through a CaringBridge Web site. Through the prayers, kind words, and visits from friends and family, Mark became encouraged. Immediately friends began composing music for one hand and two feet as well as organ duets for three hands and four feet. He did miss the funeral service for his father, which was held in Stockton on August 13. However, music from his CD was played at the service, and Mark listened to the funeral from his hospital bed via phone.

Mark began rehabilitation with challenges such as balance and phantom pains. He learned how to do daily tasks of opening jars, washing clothes, etc. Once again he was strongly driven to accomplish new goals. The incredible thing about this is that Mark didn't lose his sense of humor or sense of ministry. God has helped him enlarge his territories and minister in new ways. In addition to Mark's life being spared, miracles continued. Mark played an organ duet at his father's memorial service on November 15, 2003. A Southern California disc jockey raised over $50,000 for a new arm for him. Mark has also played at major churches in Southern California including Palm Sunday at the Crystal Cathedral, plus Good Friday and Easter at Central Assembly of God in Springfield, Missouri. Mark has not stopped his ministry nor even slowed down. Instead, his ministry is changing while he is being led by God's grace and strength. The song Mark mentioned after his accident sums it up: "Jesus is all the world to me, my life, my joy, my all. He is my strength from day to day, without Him I would fall."[1]

What I had thought was a bit "much" about Mark's passion for music turned out to be just the right amount to carry him through the pursuit of his dream, as well as the challenges after his accident. And when I stop and think about it, God gives each of us "the right amount" to carry us through each moment of our lives. Mark was driven as a young boy to achieve his dream and now continues to be driven in whatever ministry opportunities open to him.

"But he said to me, 'My grace is sufficient for you, for my power is made perfect in weakness.' Therefore I will boast all the more gladly about my weaknesses, so that Christ's power may rest on me." (2 Cor. 12:9 NIV)

Mark is joined by his cousin Joyce Pryor in front of the piano that his parents bought for him when he was in the fifth grade.

1. "Jesus Is All the World to Me" by Will L. Thompson.

Ginger Ale

by Gary DeVaul

It was the first word – on the first morning – of the first day – after the accident. Mark was, thankfully, heavily sedated that morning. Morphine was soothing a lump of flesh that had in its fifty-plus years known only the benefits of Coca-Cola. "Wow!" and "ginger ale" seemed now to be the extent of his vocabulary.

Mark didn't know it, but morphine makes you thirsty. And, boy, was he thirsty! At first I swabbed his mouth with ice because we weren't at all sure he could swallow. We were wrong. He could. And soon enough, he let us know it. The nurse told me that there was a kitchen for ambulatory patients and visitors alike just outside the door of Mark's room and that in that kitchen there was Diet Sprite, regular Sprite, and ginger ale. "No Coke?" a thin little voice whispered. "No Coke," the nurse replied. "Oh, wow." Back to sleep. Then I heard it. It's all I heard for hours. "Ginger ale," he said. "What?" I replied. Now, more clearly, bubbling up from the cauldron of Markish mirth to the all-too-sad surface was a little smile, just a hint of the impish humor I had missed for too many hours. "Ginger ale!" he repeated. Okay, okay, ginger ale it is! And I was off on the first of many visits to the kitchen to fetch ginger ale.

Well, I found the little kitchen, discovered the dispenser, the cups, and ice, and noticed that there was Diet Sprite as well. I thought I'd indulge myself, as the sight of Mark's dry lips was making me thirsty, too. I poured the ginger ale and dispensed a cup of Diet Sprite, stopped to thank the nurse at the nurses' station, and, without knowing it, mixed the darn things up. Well, for me confusion is a normal state of mind, so one shouldn't be surprised.

However, I didn't get away with my mixing mistake. Even though this kid was doped up like a drunken prizefighter, when I held the diet drink to his parched lips, he got that curious, rather twisted look on his face, took one swallow lest he die of thirst, and queried, "What is that? Poison?" I replied, "No, it's ginger ale." "It is not!" Mark said, mocking me. "It's something else. You're trying to poison me because I wrecked your car." That was the beginning of our first day of recovery. The stage was set.

I had come to the hospital early in the morning after a tossing, sleepless night. I admit I was draggin' – about as down as I could get. My heart was broken. Every time I looked at my buddy, tears of sorrow would burn just beneath the surface. Our friend Jeremy McElroy, who often performed with Mark at the organ console, would not arrive for another day, and frankly I was a quart low on comfort. Mark's sense of humor changed all that in an instant. I had not attempted to poison him. But he reached through the dopey, confused haze in which he found himself and provided the antidote he knew I needed. That was his first act of mercy to me – a sure indication that he would transform the room and the experience we were about to have with that wonderful, whimsical, dusty, dry sense of humor. A sense of humor that would sustain all whom he touched throughout this awful ordeal. More importantly, it was the tip-off that the Holy Spirit was present and doing His healing, transforming work.

I would make a lot of Mark's sense of humor in the coming few weeks, but not enough. Not nearly enough. Because this humor points us all to a fresh perspective. A perspective born out of God's grace. Humor, I am convinced, is a by-product of grace. It can use any vehicle to do its bidding. Be it ginger ale, bedpans, or belches. Grace knows no boundaries of custom, manners, or cultural norms. Not at least when it's filtered through Mark Thallander's brand of brain.

As you read these missives, I fear you will come away with the idea that we spent most of our time in the hospital, in rehab, and at home in laughter. You know what? You're right. We did. Mark,

Jeremy, John West (another organist friend who came to visit from California), and I literally spent hours laughing. Laughing until we had tears in our eyes. Laughing because it was right next to crying. But the better choice. And why not? Because we're Christians? Because people rarely laughed in the Bible? Because this was a serious, life-threatening, life-changing tragedy? Or because, like they used to say to me when I was a kid caught laughing in church, "it's disrespectful to God"? Well, that's baloney.

The New Testament clearly states that "no one will take your joy away from you" (John 16:22b). And it was Jesus' hope and prayer that "My joy may be in you, and that your joy may be made full" (John 15:11b). Years ago I took the time to count how often the word *chara,* which means "joy," is used in the New Testament. As I remember, it was fifty-eight times! Hurrah! Believe it or not! The word *chairein,* which translates "rejoice," is used seventy-three times!

Personally, I happen to nourish a curious affinity for the many insights available to us in the Creation story. The theology of the *imago dei* found in the first chapter of Genesis telegraphs to me that if we are created in the image of God, and we are, then we have within us the internal, endemic, compulsion to laugh. And if the situation forges the opportunity, then we had better do the godly thing and laugh.

For the past hundred years, psychologists from Frankl to Freud, from Menninger to Messinger, have prescribed laughter as a paramount agent of healing. Diplomats call upon its cathartic powers to ease tensions between nations. Good parents use it with children. Good doctors with patients. But the preachers and teachers of the church of the One who exemplifies it? Well, there aren't enough sermons preached on the subject of humor. The importance of a well-developed sense of humor is too often neglected. Mark lost his arm and his father in the same week. The hospital's pharmacy prescribed morphine for his body. Laughter came on the wings of angels, directly from the pharmacy of the

Great Physician to soothe and comfort the souls in need. Did we
overdose? I don't think so.

Remember Abraham and Sarah? Sarah and Abraham lived
pre-Viagra, and Sarah laughed when she was told by God that
she would conceive and have a child. Why? She laughed because
she and Abraham were antiquities. Yeah, well, what happened?
She had the child, and God named the child Isaac, which means
laughter! Sense of humor? Give me a break. We have a God in
whom humor finds its origin. If you don't believe it, just think of
the giraffe!

In Matthew 15:22-28, Jesus is in a conversation with a woman,
which of course He was not supposed to do. Why? Because good
Jewish boys didn't talk to women. Especially Canaanite women.
And in this conversation we can detect banter between the two. A
humor that's inescapable if you listen for it. The disciples came to
Jesus and said that there's a woman who is crying, her daughter is
possessed with demons, and she wants to talk to You. And Jesus
said I can't talk to her now, and anyway she's not a Jew, and I was
sent to minister to the Jews! It wouldn't be fair to give the bread
that was meant for the Jews to the Gentiles. Well, can you believe
it? The woman argued with Jesus. She said that indeed it was fair!
"Yes, Lord, but even the dogs feed on the crumbs which fall from
their masters' table" (v. 27). Now get this. Don't miss it. You
can see the smile emerge on Jesus' face. Jesus turned on a dime,
and you can almost hear Him chuckle, amused at the wonderful,
faithful persistence of the woman. He responded, "O woman, your
faith is great; it shall be done for you as you wish" (v. 28). And the
woman's daughter was healed. Grace.

What do we have here? God's grace faithfully at work in a
compassionate, mirth-filled, loving Jesus. Do you question the use
of the word *mirth* in relationship to Jesus? If so, just check your
thesaurus. *Mirth's* brother is *miraculous*. Jesus patiently heard the
truth from this woman. He responded immediately by cutting
through a raft of ancient Jewish laws based on exclusivism. He not

only heard her plea, He acted decisively and healed her daughter.
It was a huge thing for Him to do. An act fraught with religious/
political problems, and He did it, I believe, with a smile on His
face.

When Mark's father passed away and Mark's brother, Wayne,
called to tell us the tough news, we were sitting on the bed in the
hospital. Mark's face lost its color, and tears not far away vowed to
well. You know what he said to me? He looked at me with those
warm, moist, impudent eyes, smiled his sweetest smile, and said,
"Ginger ale." Off to the kitchen! More grace!

When times get tough, and do they ever, it behooves us all to
bear witness to our friend's humor. Humor is more than just a way
to circumvent problems. It is far more than the pop-psychologist's
hypothesis of denial. It faces truth head-on with a rare and
rawboned brand of courage. A courage bathed in the blood of
the One we love, plucked from the heart of Jesus. A courage that
makes life more than a possibility. It makes it an adventure in the
pleasure of being alive. It offers us a new perspective and helps us
see the world, not through the prism of tragedy, of lost arms, or
lost legs, or broken hearts, but in the light of Him who at Creation
looked at all He had made and said, "It is good, it is very good."
Good humor is a sure sign of God's grace. With a healthy quart of
ginger ale to boot!

it is a shaft of light shining
through a crack in a dark room's door
it stands between us and our sin
a line of light drawn on the floor of our soul

it is born out of love
softens blows
feathers sorrow's bed
so that deep wounds can heal

it is our divine champion when
the enemy's breath is hot
it is solace when we fail
generous in victory

it makes love palpable
forces us to consider others
under pressure it grows flesh
on the bones of courage

it stands when beauty enters the room
it muffles our anger
transforms it into active love
and petitions for a second chance

it allows us to participate in the sorrows
of the world and laugh at death's dark mask
it is that hidden burst of energy
pushing the runner through the ribbon

it is forgiveness's formula
makes one's own reflection bearable
it draws us back from perfection
to renewed perfection

it is present when laughter and tears
collide in heaven's lab
the most precious gift of God
its name is Grace.

Compassion

by Gary DeVaul

On the second day of Mark's hospitalization, a nurse's aide came into his room. She asked me to get Mark up and around, so she could put clean sheets on his bed. He needed them both, the clean sheets and a walk, but he didn't see it that way. The morphine was making bed the more comfortable choice, and when I would try to stand him up, he would get dizzy and unsteady and want to slide back under the covers. The walking thing didn't appeal to him at all. Nevertheless, he was a good patient. When the nurses – who were angels of the highest order in heaven and on earth – reminded Mark that his circulation demanded that he "move it," well, he did.

As we were creeping down the hall, he was naturally wobbly, and I, of course, was supposed to be the tugboat. Mary, a nurse, passed us by, heading the other direction. She had one of those twinkles that lives in one's heart and is reflected in one's eyes. Mary stopped just behind us and said in a mocking authoritative voice, "Mr. Thallander, why are you creeping along like that? There's nothing wrong with your legs, man. Come on, move it!" And would you believe that Mark turned, looked at her, and cocked his head toward me as if to say it was my fault? Mary, being of Irish decent, replied under her breath as she walked away, "Oh, the devil you say . . ."

When we arrived back at the room exhausted from our marathon, the nurse's assistant was finished with her bed making. She took one look at Mark and said, "Honey, we have to do something about that 'do." Being rather, shall we say, of another generation, I had no idea what a 'do was. But Mark did. "What's wrong with my hair?" he responded. And she said with fresh compassion in a voice which comes from one in touch with healing powers, "Your hair isn't black, is it, Mark?" And he replied, "No, it isn't. It's blond." "Come on," she said. "Get into bed. I'll wash your hair."

She was back in a flash with a long, funny-looking tub that fit under his head and cradled his neck. As she began to soap and scrub his hair, the water in the long tub became pink and soon turned to red. Very carefully the young woman covered the tub with a towel, so it would not frighten Mark as she removed it. In her compassion she wanted to spare him the sight. Well, it was a bit much for me. Not the blood, but the display of compassion. I headed off down the hall to get a ginger ale for the man getting the 'do in the beauty salon in room 317 . . . and to get myself together as well.

When we see true compassion, we know it and we are touched. Why? Because compassion touches. That night, after a late dinner, I was too tired to sleep. Jeremy had not arrived as yet to take the night shift, so I stole into Mark's room to check on him. Mary, the nurse, was sitting up asleep in a chair beside Mark's bed with her hand clasped in his. Mary was off duty.

Mark's insurance would not provide for a private room. Yet somehow the nurses saw to it that no one was ever scheduled for the bed next to his. These were the kind of serendipities that met us along the way. I don't use the word *blessing* very often. I think we tend to overuse it. "Oh, what a blessing" tends to fall too easily off our lips. But these were blessings in the true sense of the word. Blessings rooted in compassion.

Now for a surprise! The singular translation of the Hebrew word for *compassion,* or the corresponding word *mercy* as it is used in the Old Testament, is the word *womb!* Can you believe it? In Exodus 22:27b Yahweh says to one in need, "And if he cries to me, I will hear, for I am compassionate" (RSV). There is a good example of the flavor of the word in Jesus' statement in Luke 6:36: "Be merciful, just as your Father is merciful." The word *compassionate* had a womblike quality to it for the Hebrew listener. The womb is creative, nourishing, life-giving, safe, and all-encompassing. It is related to Jesus' intimate description of His Father which is translated "Papa." One cannot escape the tender mercies of God and the feminine side of God's nature as well, for the womblike word *compassion* completes the *imago dei,* or "image of God," as both male and female. Jesus represents the ideal in His lament, "O Jerusalem, Jerusalem, . . . How often I wanted to gather your children together, just as a hen gathers her brood under her wings" (Luke 13:34).

This compassion was the touchstone of Jesus' image of His Father, and He echoed this compassion by making it the hallmark of His ministry on earth. It is when we see compassion reflected in the lives of others, through a word, or touch, or kindness done, that we witness the vibrant living Spirit of God at work in the heart of another. This is why we are apt to be moved when some act of mercy or kindness is done to us while we are captured by a critical moment or circumstance. The Spirit within reacts to the corresponding Spirit in another – and the child leaps in the womb of John the Baptist's mother at the sight of Mary with child.

When Jesus healed, He often touched. And, believe me, He did it at great risk. Oh, not risk of infection, or of the communication of disease, but at risk of offending Jewish custom and law. For Jewish custom and law forbade touching the sick. They were seen as unclean. And being superstitious, they believed that sickness pointed to sin. Well, Jesus would have none of this first-century political correctness.

In Mark 1:40-45 a man comes to Jesus riddled with leprosy. Leprosy was the epitome of the unclean in the chronicles of Jewish tradition. Leprosy turned the flesh white, sores and ulcers appeared and ruptured, and soon the flesh rotted off. We have no idea what the noisome face of the leper looked like when he came to Jesus. But we do know that in Luke's account of the same story, the leper fell on his face to hide his shame. But Jesus saw no shame. Only agony.

Here we see the heart of Jesus in His response to suffering, for there was no greater suffering on earth than that which leprosy imposed. Jesus looked upon this wreck of humanity. He was "moved with compassion" (v. 41). He reached out and "touched him" (v. 41), instantly healing the leprosy and shattering the ancient taboo. We see one more act of compassion on Jesus' part to the leper, now healed. He did not want the man to bear the penalty for a law broken by Divinity. So He sent the man to the high priest to show himself as clean, as the Law of Moses required.

Phantom pain is very real to the sufferer. Mark can feel the fingernails bite into the palm of his left hand. The missing arm and hand often cramp and curl under his chest. The pain can be unbearable at times. Toward the end of Mark's stay at Maine Medical Center, a physical therapist met with him to aid in his recovery. The young woman had a deep understanding of Mark's pain and a compassion that outweighed her understanding. She asked Mark to close his eyes and concentrate on a white light. Mark was reminded of the light he saw in his near-death experience with morphine. He said that he had been drawn up through a tunnel of light and angels literally sent him back to us. While Mark was meditating on this very same light, the therapist moved the palm of her hand over his invisible arm and hand in a comforting, soothing motion. Soon I saw an expression of joy sweep over Mark's face as the phantom pain lessened. "I can feel the warmth of your hand," Mark commented. "I can move my fingers. My hand is opening up. Oh, wow, I can feel the cool air between my fingers." The therapist's face mirrored the joy of Mark's expression. The whole room took on a quality of radiance. Personally I have never experienced anything like that moment. The healing time found its essence in a woman who knew God's love and engendered God's compassion. Thus are His servants at Maine Medical Center.

It is this same compassion, and no less, that has swelled the trust fund for Mark and made it possible for him to live, pay his bills, and put his life back together. Your contributions are just as meaningful as the hand holding his in the darkness of night. From the bottom of his heart to the top of his blond head, he thanks you. When the angel asks with mocking mirth, "Mr. Thallander, what are you doing up and about so soon?" he simply turns and nods his head towards you. For you are to blame. "Oh, the devil you say . . ."

In the Hands of Angels

by Gary DeVaul

The 4Runner was resting on its passenger side. Glass, dirt, rain, and blood, its metallic mess. Mark partially hanging by the seat belt, but mostly supporting himself with his right arm against the passenger door. Covered with glass, yet never cut, Mark was conscious and thinking a hundred miles a minute. Odd how when we are in desperate peril, time goes so slowly. Or is it that our brain's synaptic powers increase rapidly and conscious thought outruns normal time and space? I'm not sure. But I am sure that it is the Creator's way of helping us to purchase balance and save ourselves while in harm's way. It is one of the angels of our nature implanted in our very genes. But there are other angels . . .

A voice is heard over the wreckage. "Are you okay? Tell me who you are. No, no, keep talking. I've called the paramedics, and they'll be here soon. See if you can turn off the engine. No, no, keep talking – they'll need your help when they arrive. Can you unbuckle the seat belt?" Mark has said time and time again, "I never saw her. I'm almost sure it was a woman standing there in the rain talking to me, but I couldn't see her. She wouldn't let me slip into unconsciousness. I've tried to find out her identity through the police and the paramedics; yet it appears that when they arrived, she was gone! She may have saved my life, and I want to thank her. It was because she kept me conscious that I was able to turn off the car engine in order to avoid a fire. It was because she kept me awake that I had the sense to thrust my good hand into my left shoulder and keep myself from bleeding to death." My oldest son, Grant, heard Mark tell the story over lunch last Sunday.

He said, "Mark, I know who that was, and so do you. It was an angel." Grant is right. It takes one to know one.

Gary's Toyota 4Runner after Mark's accident

It's been three days of morphine since that fateful accident. It sounds a bit like Mark is snoring, but more than that. It stops, it starts, it's loud, then gulping, and then gurgling. Paul, a nurse at another hospital, walks in to say hello and at once recognizes the sounds of approaching death. He calls for help. Mark is saved again. Angels.

It's the fourth morning. Word has spread quickly throughout the Christian community. One of ours is wounded. A sea of flowers arrives at a hospital not acquainted with this kind of celebrity. The room fills fast. There are no window ledges left, the dressers are covered, and soon the whole third floor becomes the beneficiary of flowers sent on angels' wings. The letters, cards, and e-mails build day upon day until the hospital cries for mercy and we have to shut down the phone in Mark's room. And how, I ask, does one count your petitions? How many pleas can the prayer waves accommodate?

Oh yeah, this guy is strong. He comes from Norwegian stock. These were the guys who conquered Britain and ruled the seas, discovered the New World, the Vikings of old. And then the doctors say, "Oh, Mark, this is good. You are healing well and very fast." And Mark replies, "By the way, where'd you put my arm? I hope you froze it. We'll need it in order to create a model for the new one." The doctor rolls his eyes in disbelief, stymied by a sense of humor that's fed by prayers and e-mails and cards and flowers and phone calls, from angels far and wide. Angels all.

Angels have more than wings, you know. They have hands. Hands that cut steel, lift glass, wipe tears, wash bodies, sign checks, write letters, and cut seat belts and save. Angels have hands that heal and pray, and stand in the darkness, and call for help in the rain, and steady, and comfort, and watch, until help arrives a second time. All these hands have one redeeming value, one priceless mark of identification. Ask St. Thomas what it is.

Never before has it been so perfectly clear to me that God lives in each of us and we in Him. It is an idea that is too often overlooked; yet it is a major theme in Christian conscious thought. "And the Word became flesh" (John 1:14a). Emmanuel! It doesn't just happen at Christmas when we are marketed into it by hymns and lights and preachers. No, it's not just words on a page, or the opening of John's gospel. Theologians have argued, waged wars, fought, and died over this idea that the elements of the Eucharist become via "accident" the very body and blood of Christ.

Oh my, what a waste of time. The body of Christ stands behind the altar, it sits in the pew, it responds to calamity and confusion with scared but steady hands. These are the hands of angels, and do you know to whom they belong? They belong to you. Oh, don't be embarrassed to think about it. Your hands have become God's hands. It's called incarnation. It didn't just happen in the Book; it happens every day. Look there! See the scars, the marks of love.

Need more proof? Guess what? Mark's coming home! His shoulder is healing, his heart is mending, his eyes are clearer than ever before. He carries in his breast a confidence that shatters obstacles like so much crystal on a marble floor. He awoke the other day to tell me that he had arranged the hymn "O for a Thousand Tongues to Sing" for one hand and two feet. He has also rearranged his Toccata on "Hymn to Joy" for one hand and two feet! You know what? You're going to hear him play again!

There'll be a day in the near future – you wait and see. I'll be there. You'll be there. He will walk onto the stage, or into the chancel, with one hand, and the organ will thunder and sing as if he had two. Jesus' eyes will fill with tears, and you will take out your handkerchief. Angels will jump to their feet in applause, and your hands will sting with joy. Someone will turn to you before the finale and whisper, "I can't tell the difference. Sounds like he's playing with two hands." And you will turn and say, "He is! The second hand is yours!" Angels all . . .

Nursed Back to Health

by Mark Thallander

Four surgeons at Maine Medical Center (MMC) were awaiting the arrival of the ambulance from Wells Emergency Services. Because of the intense weather, I was unable to be airlifted from the Wells turnpike entrance to the hospital in Portland, Maine, some forty miles away. As I was being transported, the doctors were preparing for probable surgery. And I was informing the ambulance attendant that I was an organist. Although I did not know my left arm had been pulled out of its socket, I remember communicating with him that I needed both arms for my career. Upon arrival at the emergency room, I was asked to sign papers giving my permission to amputate, if necessary.

I requested that Gary DeVaul be notified immediately. However, my cell phone, with Gary's number, was still in the wrecked vehicle. I was told that the hospital personnel were unable to reach Gary because his number was unlisted. I directed them to call the Ogunquit Police Department (as a police officer could drive to Gary's home and notify him) and also to try Ron, a friend of Gary's in nearby Kennebunkport. Thankfully, Ron's number was listed. I requested that the surgeons wait for Gary's arrival before I was taken into the operating room. But there wasn't time. My life was hanging in the balance. The anesthesiologist introduced himself. I knew now that in a matter of seconds I would be under.

So I put myself into the merciful hands and everlasting arms of God and was rolled down the hallway into surgery. Little did I realize just how much I would be leaning on those everlasting arms in the weeks, months, and years to come.

I was later informed that Ron was able to reach Gary just as the police were pulling into Gary's driveway. Since Gary's Toyota 4Runner was totaled, Ron drove to Ogunquit to get Gary, and they both arrived at the medical center while I was in the recovery room.

For the next week, the surgeons visited me very early every morning in room 317. MMC is also a teaching hospital, which meant medical students were often alongside the doctors. The nurses and certified nursing assistants – Wendy, Mary, Brian, Paul, Jeremy, Michael, and many others – were remarkable. Some stayed by my side long after their shifts were completed. On one occasion, a nurse stayed an extra two hours, keeping me company and massaging my feet with a special lotion he had located on another floor. Even after I was moved to New England Rehabilitation Hospital (NERH), some of these dedicated caregivers visited me there and also encouraged me with messages they posted on my CaringBridge Web site.

As a medical student working on Mark's team, I've had the privilege of being involved in his care since he came in last Sunday. It's been wonderful getting to know the man who was initially hidden under the effects of pain medications, and seeing what a courageous and kind person he is. While I wish he were here under different circumstances, I feel lucky to have had the opportunity to meet him, and I'm delighted to see such an outpouring of love from so many people close to him. We all wish him the greatest of luck once he leaves Maine Medical Center, and will never forget him.
Ariana W.
Portland, ME

Hello, Mark, Just a quick note of appreciation for today's journal entry and hopes that all is going well at New England Rehab. I hold you in my thoughts and prayers. You are a WONDER!!
Judith B., Chaplain, Maine Medical Center
Portland, ME

Mark, you inspire me. You make me glad that I became a nurse. Mary agrees and sends hello and best wishes.
Kathy RN from Maine Medical Center
Portland, ME

Mark,
You're looking absolutely fabulous! I'm Brian, one of the CNAs on R3 at Maine Medical Center. We all had great empathy for you, but just as we knew you'd be right back on top! I am amazed and encouraged by your tremendous support system. I only got to see you and Jeremy as I only worked nights and missed the opportunity of meeting your other wonderful friends that were there during the day. Believe me though, many of us walking through the door into work each and every night had to get our "Mark update" before anything else. . . . It's obvious you are surrounded by loving, wonderful people. It was unfortunate the way we met, but I feel privileged to have known you. I wish you and yours all the best!
Brian V.
Portland, ME

Hi Mark,
It's Michael writing, the C.N.A that took care of you in the hospital. I just looked down through the updates of what's going on with you over the past few weeks/month since we parted at the hospital. I'm so glad to see you're doing so well, though I knew that a person with such great strength, and courage, as well as the circle of faith and friendship that with life's bumps and curves you would pick up in no time and be well on your way with new adjustments in your life. MAY THE LORD WALK BESIDE YOU EACH AND EVERY DAY. I'm so thankful to have met you, and all your friends, especially Gary and Jeremy. You two guys are absolutely "Angels from Heaven," and I'm so proud of you both, as well as having the pleasure, and a true pleasure indeed to have met you. "May peace forever be with you both." I believe it's in the love of our friendship through GOD as well as with GOD that we are given the strength to go on as you have. I'm sorry it

*has been this long since I've written to you, though you have been in
my thoughts and prayers daily. I'm truly glad to hear that you're doing
so well in your recovery. Gary and Jeremy have taken such great care
of you, as with the love and support of MANY others. GOD BLESS
YOU MARK. You have inspired me in so many ways. PEACE BE
WITH YOU ALWAYS!*

Michael R.
Maine Medical Center
Portland, ME

An old gospel song asks the question, Will your anchor hold
in the storms of life? The hymn writer's refrain responds with this
affirmation:

> *We have an anchor that keeps the soul*
> *Steadfast and sure while the billows roll,*
> *Fastened to the Rock which cannot move,*
> *Grounded firm and deep in the Savior's love.*[1]

What a network of prayer surrounded me around the clock.
What a privilege to be a part of the family of God. Spiritually, I
was surrounded by family, friends, pastors, professors, phone calls,
e-mails, cards, flowers – God used the love and prayers of thousands
of people to encourage me in a way I never dreamed possible.

And He used the excellent care provided by MMC and then
NERH. With my transfer to the rehab hospital, I was put under
the gifted care of occupational therapist Annette, physical therapist
Greg, and weekend therapist Carolyn. Each morning these
dedicated people presented me with my grueling schedule for the
day. After my release from rehab, I received outpatient therapy
from Stephán at York Hospital in York, Maine. From Portland
to York, these committed professionals all significantly assisted in
continuing the process of nursing me back to health!

1. "We Have an Anchor" by Priscilla Jane Owens.

Heart Struck

by Gary DeVaul

Being heart struck takes place when one goes to the essence of a person, problem, or possibility and hits the mark.

"Read to me." It was a litany. "Read to me." Between taking medicine, sleeping, eating, washing, changing bandages, and talking to doctors and nurses, it was, "Read to me." And what did Mark want read? Well, in the first few days after his accident, there were hundreds of e-mails to the hospital. Then came the get well cards. Over seven hundred cards arrived! Mark counted them, or he had me count them. I don't remember. He had Jeremy and me read every one of them to him because it was too difficult for him to open envelopes with one hand. Mark is famous for his fastidious organizational skills. He's the kind of guy who lines up his socks in the drawer according to size and color. He makes the likes of me crazy! Lists were compiled of who sent what. The cards were filed and organized and laid out on the adjoining bed. Jeremy and I sometimes felt like the bride's mother taking notes at a bridal shower. Oh, this guy drove me nuts! I mean this kind of attention to detail gives me the whim-whams! But the really hard part for me was reading.

Oh, don't worry, I can read. I've become an Episcopalian! It's what the angels wrote that made it impossible for me to read. Remember now, Mark and I were forged in the crucible of Possibility Thinking! But this task was too much. The tears would come. The throat would tighten. The voice would choke and break. Oh, I was a mess! So Jeremy got the job because Jeremy is made of tough stuff. The poor kid read till his reader broke!

Kidding aside, the letters, flowers, cards, and e-mails were like a balm to Mark's soul. He devoured them. And they nourished him. After Mark was released from the rehabilitation center, we kept them in a huge basket in my living room, and "Read to me" became the mantra of the day. But there was another source of healing to be found.

We didn't want Mark to be alone. And because I'm in the very grip of antiquity, Jeremy took the night shift. He slept on a cot in Mark's room for over a week. And every night the two of them did what many of us talk about but few do, me included. Every night they had their devotional time. Prayers were said, Scripture was read, sometimes they sang, and an enormous comfort filled the room. These guys struck at the heart of the healing process. They went to the temple within. But then, they had a good model.

It was Passover. Thousands of Israelites flooded the Holy City to visit the temple, pray, make their sacrifices, and mix and talk with old friends. They feasted and danced together. You can bet that it was a good time. Jesus, too, decided to make His pilgrimage to Jerusalem.

Here, He came on a small donkey, riding in triumph. There was great joy! The very rocks were bound to burst into song! The palms and people were in celebration together! But there's a subterranean message here that goes far beyond the celebration we accord Palm Sunday and Passover. Jesus was not pleased, to put it mildly. His pilgrimage into the Holy City was a not-too-subtle stab at the heart of the establishment. He was mocking the generals, the potentates, and the clergy. For they all had their fine horses, and they came in parades of colorful robes, rapt in self-glorification.

But Jesus' progress was on an ass. And in doing so, he made one out of the establishment. You see, He was angry. In his gospel, Mark writes that Jesus had visited the temple the night before. He witnessed the desecration of the Court of the Gentiles. He saw the animals and the moneychangers. He heard the noise and smelled the perversion. The Court of the Gentiles, the very place created to be a witness to the glory of God to all nations, had become a meat market. Jesus' heart was broken. John writes in his gospel that Jesus went back to Bethany that night and made a "whip of cords" (John 2:15 RSV) with which to clear out the mess. Call it righteous indignation if you will, but Jesus was planning a strike at the heart.

He was exasperated with the laws of exclusivity that separated people into categories, laws that measured every man by the bottom line of his ledger and measured women not at all, for they were counted with the cattle and sheep. He could have been tired of seeing the blood flow from the altar of the temple, the red flood running down the culverts from the altar to the floor and into the stinking streets below, streets filled with disease, and flies, and vermin. Thousands of sacrifices were being made. The animals filled the yard. The pilgrims were not allowed to bring their own. They were required to buy them in the temple yard. The moneychangers were there because only a special coin could be used to purchase an animal for sacrifice. And usury was rampant. One sacrifice could easily cost a man a day's wages.

Jesus' heart was in rebellion. He chose to live with tax collectors, eat with the sick and dying, and talk with women of every forbidden tribe and region. He touched the untouchable lepers. He healed the blind with His own spit and lifted the dead from their graves. And if need be, He would break the Law of Moses to save a life or comfort the anguished. Jesus was a radical, and He was heartsick at the sight of His Father's house of prayer being turned into a sideshow for the rich and famous.

Armed with the whip and the support of His followers, Jesus struck! He must have been ferocious. The tables were overturned! People, money, and animals fled or were dashed to the floor! The temple guards, whose responsibility it was to secure the holy place, were obviously too intimidated by Jesus and His followers to stop the rebellion. The Gospels don't even mention them. But Mark writes that the chief priests and scribes were furious and they plotted to kill Jesus (Mark 11:18). Annas, the former high priest, was in charge of the buying and selling. It was one thing to make

fools of the priesthood and undermine their authority. It was quite
another to hit their pocketbooks. Jesus knew that He would pay
with His life. He also knew that all the ills of Israel were nurtured
from the spiritual center of the city, and He struck at the heart and
sealed His fate.

The story is about striking at the heart of the problem, which
Jesus clearly recognized as the realm of the spiritual. If the Spirit's
candle burned bright, all the darkness and death in the universe
could not prevail. He could have marched on Pilate's palace or
shaken Herod's throne. He could have protested in the streets
before the Roman guard. Instead, He chose the temple.

We knew that Mark's father had fallen the night of Mark's
accident. We knew his heart was failing and that a breathing
machine was all that kept him from the gates of heaven. The
family had vowed not to let his suffering continue. They decided
to remove the machine. They waited a day in order to honor Mark's
birthday. The life support would be removed on August 10, Mark's
brother's birthday, instead. I will never forget the calm with which
Mark faced the phone call from his brother, Wayne. Mark and
Jeremy had visited the temple the night before.

The Court of the Gentiles was clean and clear! The Holy of
Holies stood open to him, for the curtain had been torn from top to
bottom by the One who had gone before. The call from California
finally came. There was grief and sorrow, but also a quiet sense of
celebration. The angel of death and darkness had passed over and
had found no place to rest.

After a time of quiet, I found Mark serene and composed. He
was sitting at the computer next to his bed. He had just finished
planning the funeral service for his father. I put a cup of ginger ale
on the bed stand and asked Mark if there was anything that I could
do for him. He smiled and said, "Read to me."

Trust and Obey

by Paul Bandy

There are times for each of us when something happens that has a profound impact on our lives. Under the word *profound* the *Merriam-Webster's Collegiate Dictionary* lists: "difficult to fathom or understand; extending far below the surface; coming from, reaching to, or situated at a depth; characterized by intensity of feeling or quality; all encompassing." All of those descriptions applied to my feelings upon hearing about Mark's accident and the unthinkable consequence of the loss of his left arm, and they apply to what has happened since.

On Sunday evening, August 3, 2003, I had just returned home from a wonderful four-day Christian conference in San Diego, California, when I received the call from a friend that Mark had been in an accident in Maine, was in critical condition, and had lost his left arm. I went through the usual stages of stunned disbelief, grief, and sympathy for my friend. It was hard to wrap my mind around how this could happen to someone who was so gifted and had dedicated his life to serving God through music. Music was his life! What would he do now?

The next stage for me was: What can I do to help? I spent some time in prayer for Mark directly and also asked that God would use me in some way to help. Then I started making calls to friends and churches Mark had served, asking them to put him on their prayer lists to pray for his recovery. Since Mark and I lived in the same building, I had been collecting his mail for the many weeks he had been on his playing tour and vacation to the East Coast and Canada that summer. He originally had been scheduled to fly home to California in early August. I knew he had bills due, so I sorted his mail and went through the bills. His car and medical insurance premiums were due, and I knew those had to be paid. I received calls from several friends asking how they could help. One couple sent a check to me for $500 and another for $250 to meet the immediate needs. Another friend sent a $1,000 check back to Maine to help with expenses there. This was only the beginning of the overwhelming generosity of so many wonderful people who wanted to help in some tangible way.

Prior to the accident I knew that Mark was well known and respected, but I had no idea that the response of people to his physical, emotional, spiritual, and financial needs following his loss would be so tremendous. Also, prior to the accident I had known that Mark was a deeply committed man of faith and had dedicated his life to serving God through music. I knew that he trusted in God's love and care, but I had no idea how that would be put to the test. Nor did I know how Mark would so graphically demonstrate just how strong that faith was and how God would bless so many others through Mark's great faith, trust in God's care, and ultimate plan for his life, and his obedience to follow wherever God led through this new and totally unexpected journey.

I received a call from Janelle Grose, then director of events and services at Lake Avenue Church in Pasadena, California, who said that people wanted to help Mark financially. We talked about how to make that possible. She connected me with Lois Dalke Williams and Leigh Trenham, and we later met with a lawyer to set up a trust fund to help with Mark's medical and living expenses, both in the short and long term. I did not know Lois or Leigh prior to this and had no idea what a blessing their friendships would become to me, and to many others, as we worked together to help our dear friend.

After information about the trust was published by Lake Avenue Church and other churches, it quickly became evident that God was deeply touching the lives of many people across the country through what had happened to Mark. The response was overwhelming. Again, the word *profound* comes to mind as people responded with prayers, cards, letters, e-mails, and checks. From talking with the friends who were there at the hospital and rehab with Mark in Maine, and later with Mark, I know this outpouring of prayer, love, and concern was a tremendous encouragement to Mark and that he felt it in a very real way.

A number of Mark's friends began talking about how they might be able to raise money for the trust fund. Eric Dale Knapp conceived the idea of a benefit concert with musician friends donating their time to perform and help in the production, with proceeds going to the Mark A. Thallander Trust. A concert committee was formed which included Lois Bock, Marilyn Fontana, Judy MacLeod, Frederick Swann, Leigh Trenham, John West, Lois Williams, and myself. Other people, such as Janelle Grose, contributed as well.

The first benefit concert, Affirmation of Faith and Life, was held at Lake Avenue Church in Pasadena on March 21, 2004, with David and Darlene Feit-Pretzer co-chairing the event. It was a glorious celebration of Mark's life and God's wonderful grace, with over 800 singers from 30 churches in southern and northern California and Canada participating and with over 3,800 in attendance. People were generous when the offering was taken, which gave a tremendous boost to the trust fund. Also, that wonderful experience with people from so many different Christian denominations and faith communities coming together to celebrate and worship gave birth to the vision of replicating that opportunity for people across the county to come together and experience the glory of praising God through beautiful music. That vision, and the understanding that music offers the unique opportunity for unifying the diverse Christian community, provided a new direction and ministry for Mark and led to the incorporation of the Mark Thallander Foundation in 2005.

A second benefit, the Mark Thallander Keyboard Benefit Concert, was held September 10, 2004, at the Crystal Cathedral in Garden Grove, California. Christopher Pardini and John West coordinated the event, and again, performers and others helping with the production donated their time, with the proceeds from the offering going to the Mark A. Thallander Trust.

Since that time, as Mark has grown stronger physically, he has shared his journey across the country, and others have responded with generous financial support to meet his medical and living expenses. When Mark shared in the weekend services at Lake Avenue Church, radio personality Rick Dees and his wife, Julie, were so moved by Mark's story that the next week Rick started a drive on his morning radio show to raise money for a prosthetic arm for Mark. He raised over $50,000! The generosity and response of Rick and others to the need had a deep impact on Mark and was tremendously encouraging to him as he watched God work through others, His wonders to perform.

As chair of the Trust, I can affirm that the financial generosity, prayers, cards, letters, and e-mails of hundreds of people around the country and beyond have made a profound difference in Mark's life as he continues the journey of recovery from the physical trauma his body has gone through, as well as the loss of income from not being able to work. That generosity also helps sustain him as he continues to deal with ongoing pain and adapts to his new physical limitations in daily life. Through it all, Mark continues to demonstrate a genuine and inspiring positive mental attitude which is a reflection of his deep spiritual faith and trust that God has and will continue to provide for all of his needs.

God is so good! Even in times of great tragedy in our lives God is faithful and His grace is sufficient. Mark so wonderfully demonstrates that with his tremendous faith and willingness to follow wherever God leads, on unimagined paths. Through great physical and emotional pain and loss, Mark has never lost his faith or his "wicked" sense of humor, as so many of us can testify.

To me, and many others, Mark is a true champion rising above the difficulties of life to demonstrate that we can trust God with our lives, no matter what may come. Mark is living proof of the truth in the words of the second stanza and refrain from an old gospel hymn:

> *Not a burden we bear, not a sorrow we share,*
> *But our toil He does richly repay;*
> *Not a grief or a loss, not a frown or a cross,*
> *But is blest if we trust and obey.*
> *Trust and obey, for there's no other way*
> *To be happy in Jesus, but to trust and obey.*[1]

1. "Trust and Obey" by James H. Sammis.

The Pastor Visits the Patient

by Dr. David Clark

There are some days in a person's life that remain in one's memory forever. We can remember where we were, what we were thinking and feeling, every detail. Tuesday, August 5, 2003, was one of those days for me.

It began as most other Tuesdays. After my normal morning routine, I walked across the street from my home to my office at the Ogunquit Baptist Church. Like many other pastors, I take Monday as my day off, so Tuesday is the beginning of my work week. Tuesday mornings are usually concerned with organizing my week, making appointments, acting on unfinished business from the previous Sunday, sorting through the piles of papers that accumulate on my desk, beginning my sermon preparation – usually rather a routine, unexciting morning.

On this particular Tuesday, however, I smiled to myself as I anticipated a visit from Mark Thallander. Mark had played a concert at our church a couple of weeks before and would be coming in to receive his honoraria as well as have one final visit with me before returning to California. We had become friends, beginning a couple of years before when he was visiting a good friend in our seaside village in Maine and attended a service at our church, introduced himself, and offered to play for us in exchange for practice time on our organ. Mark's summer visits became a special treat for me, and that Tuesday morning I was looking forward to having one last visit with my good friend. We would talk, laugh, insult each other (all in good fun), pray, hug, and part, looking forward to the next year.

As the morning progressed, Mark did not come. I busied myself with other things. Finally there was a knock on my office door. It wasn't Mark, but rather one of my lay leaders with a contractor who was there to look over a job we needed done and give us a bid. While talking with them, the phone rang, so I excused myself and answered it. It was Jeremy McElroy, Mark's good friend and fellow musician, who had played with Mark in the concert at our church and who had also become a good friend of mine. I mentioned to him that I was waiting for Mark to show up, and I made some stupid remark that was intended to be funny. Jeremy did not laugh. Instead, he proceeded to tell me that he had some bad news. Mark had been in an accident two days before. I asked if he was okay, and Jeremy replied that he was at Maine Medical Center in Portland. He then paused and choked out the words, "Pastor Dave, they had to amputate his left arm." Words cannot describe the level of shock I felt the moment I heard his words. It was a visceral reaction, felt deep down in my being. I pumped Jeremy for details in rapid-fire fashion, realizing only later what he must have been going through as he patiently told me what he knew.

My immediate instinct was to jump in my car and go to Mark's bedside. Wisely, Jeremy cautioned me against that, as Mark had several people already holding vigil at his bedside and needed rest, not more people hovering around him. When our conversation ended, I slumped back in my chair, oblivious to the world around me, eyes moist, and prayed the best I could. I realized that it was now my task to inform the church folks who had come to love Mark as I had and, as pastor, to offer some spiritual counsel and comfort. What could I say? I myself was devastated, with more questions than answers. Through the grace of God, I somehow managed to do that and to get myself through the day's activities.

My first opportunity to actually see Mark following his accident came a number of days later. He had been transferred to a rehab hospital in Portland, and so I went, not knowing what I would encounter nor how I would react when I first saw him. When I arrived at his room, he was not there. On the bedside table I

found the beginnings of a manuscript, written by Mark's friend and
Ogunquit resident Gary DeVaul and chronicling the day of Mark's
accident (this subsequently became the first chapter of *Champions*).
There were cards, messages, and flowers seemingly everywhere. A
nurse told me that Mark was scheduled for physical therapy and
said it would be alright if I went and saw him there. He wasn't
there when I arrived, but I was told that he would be any minute
and that I should wait.

I had tried to prepare myself for the sight of my friend minus
his left arm. I knew it would be difficult. I didn't want to stare
and certainly didn't want to look shocked or overly emotional. I
prayed for God to give me the right reaction and the proper words
to say to Mark. A couple of minutes later Mark appeared down
the hallway and came toward me, accompanied by a nurse. It was
an emotionally difficult moment for me. But Mark, as he always
does, diffused the situation with his smile, warm welcome, and bad
jokes. I told him I would wait for him in his room until his session
was completed, but he insisted that I visit with him as he was put
through his paces. We made small talk as the therapist worked
with him, Mark occasionally grimacing as she did. Typically, Mark
didn't seem to want to dwell on his situation, but rather wanted to
know about what was happening with me, my wife, the church,
etc. When the session was over, we went back to his room where
it was obvious that Mark was getting weary. We prayed and I left.
I remember feeling that the roles had been reversed. I had gone to
bring comfort and strength to him; I left feeling that he had done
that for me. He has a knack for doing that, which is one of Mark's
truly remarkable gifts.

Eventually Mark was allowed to return to Ogunquit and
continue his rehab on an outpatient basis in York before returning
home to California. On the first Sunday morning he felt well
enough to do so, he came to our church service. He wanted no
fanfare, no big deal made, but only to sit in the back and worship.
Such was not easy to pull off in a gathering of seventy people,
people who had come to know and love him and who had been

faithfully praying for him. We opened the service singing of God's faithfulness and closed it with a hymn that Mark said had helped to get him through the tough times, "Jesus Is All the World to Me." And though the service was focused on God, Mark was certainly on everyone's mind, especially mine. I preached that day with my every word and thought filtered through Mark's experience. It was an emotional day for all of us, and God was powerfully present.

Much has happened in the three years since that summer. Mark has played concerts in Ogunquit again. We have shared some wonderful times, traveling the coast of Maine, taking a sailing cruise, worshiping, laughing, and ministering together. I have moved from Ogunquit and am now serving at Court Street Baptist Church in Auburn, Maine, where I have the opportunity to introduce Mark to a whole new group of people and have him play our church's magnificent organ. I must confess that I could not have imagined back on August 5, 2003, that any of that would have been possible. I have learned and grown so much through, in a small way, being a part of the drama that has been Mark's life. He has taught me so much through his example. I am honored to be one of his many friends. As I think back on all this I am struck by two facts: God is an awesome God, and Mark is a truly remarkable man.

Mark encountered a Maine lobster while on a day trip with David and Wandah Clark.

Inside Out

by Gary DeVaul

L iving life from the inside out – versus the outside in – is
   tuff stuff to do in a world that focuses on the material and
external. But Jesus teaches that it's an imperative.

When my middle son, Matthew, was about four years old, I
saw him come downstairs one morning wearing his sweater inside
out. I remember saying, "Hey Matty, come here and let Daddy fix
your sweater." Matty couldn't pronounce the letter *R* so sweater,
became sweatuh. "What's wrong with my sweatuh, Dad?" "Well,"
I said, "you've got it on inside out, Matty." When I tried to take
it off and fix it, he began to tear up. "No, Daddy, this is the way I
like it. Can't you see it's beautiful?" So for once in my life I shut
up, and listened, and let him wear his sweatuh inside out all day.
He was happy as a clam, and the neighbors thought I was nuts!
Could it be?

Matthew's little spirit made its choice based on an awareness
of a certain template of beauty on the inside that he wanted to
reflect on the outside. Today, Matthew is thirty, he can pronounce
the letter *R*, and his awareness of the Spirit within has grown and
developed. It sometimes displays itself in beautiful paintings that
flow from his hand. Those paintings come from the inside out.

When Mark was recuperating in Ogunquit, Maine, a group
of people he hadn't seen for some time came to visit. Mark was
upstairs in his room dressing. And, of course, dressing takes Mark
twice as long today as it did prior to his accident. The guests were
stewing downstairs. They were not quite sure how to greet him.
They were understandably nervous. Do they hug him? What
happens if they begin to cry? How would that make him feel?

They certainly wouldn't want to laugh. The tension was building. We were standing together in the kitchen when he finally appeared. He looked wonderful in his freshly pressed pants and shirt. He took one passing glance at everyone in the room and said to me, "Gary, I'm all dressed up, but I can't go out like this. What have you done with my arm?" "Oh, Mark," I replied, "it's in the freezer. You'll have to go without it." The tension exploded in laughter. The hugs and kisses and tears were allowed to take their course, and all because Mark had disarmed (as he would put it) the room. The Spirit within him rushed to the rescue as it sensed the agony of others. That's an example of living life inside out.

Now, don't get crazy regarding what I'm about to write next. Just hold on. Hang in there and read: Mark is a Spirit Person. He's aware of the Spirit within, and Mark lets Him flow from the inside out. That's why we love Mark. Jesus was the ultimate Spirit Person – and Him we adore. Why? It's because you can see the face of God in Spirit People, the face we saw in Eden.

God's Spirit was bestowed on all of us at creation. In Genesis 2:7, God molds and makes Adam, whose name translated literally means man or mankind. He makes Adam out of the dust of the earth. After He has fashioned him perfectly in His own image, He breathes the breath of life into Adam's nostrils, and in that instant we are alive! But what makes humankind alive? God's Spirit! Do all human beings have God's Spirit within? Absolutely, well, all of the living ones anyway! Remember, the words *breath, wind, air,* and *spirit* are all the same word in Hebrew. And Adam wasn't animated and alive until God's very Spirit was present within him.

What makes a Spirit Person, a Spirit Person? It's the continuing progressive awareness that God is the Life Force within. To cast the point in concrete, check out Genesis 6:3. "My Spirit shall not strive with man forever, because he also is flesh . . . " When the flesh gives out, and it will, the Spirit of God lives on; He never gives out.

When Jesus' flesh crumbled on the cross, His last words were to give His Spirit – which was God's already – back to God. Jesus' awareness of the Spirit of God within was so highly developed that we can witness incarnation, God in the flesh, when we look upon Him. Surprisingly, nowhere in the Gospels does Jesus ask to be worshiped. No, you look and see. Not once. But He does ask to be followed. He asks to be imitated. Jesus spent long hours in prayer and meditation. Why? He wanted to keep in touch with the powerful, creative, and dynamic Spirit within. He was constantly, consistently, developing His awareness and living His life from the inside out, not the outside in. Why do we worship Him? Because the Spirit within us rises up and adores the Spirit within Him. And in worship we are encouraged to develop that wonderful personal awareness of the Spirit within.

After the crash that made my buddy the man he is today, it was my task to call those closest to Mark and inform them of the accident and the amputation. Those were the hardest calls I've ever made. Why? Because I knew the level of devastation and grief that would follow would match the love so many bear for him all over the world. And why is he loved? It is because he tries harder than most to develop his awareness of the Spirit within, and he does his best to live his life from the inside out. We recognize the face of God when we observe one living from the inside out and the Spirit within us rises up to revel and embrace its own.

The call I made that morning was to Jeremy McElroy. I heard the silence of disbelief on the line and then the heartbreaking timbre of his sobs as his voice choked and cracked. I heard his deep shuttering breaths as he struggled to remain centered, so that he could fathom and respond with grace. It was a short call; its brevity all we two could bear.

During the call, we decided to have Jeremy contact John West who loves Mark and is well connected. John sent an e-mail to a powerful list of Spirit People, and literally thousands of you responded within moments. Why? Because the Spirit within you responds to one who lives his life inside out.

What does it mean to live from the inside out? It means that we are beginning to understand that in Christ we are all one. And it means that there is a growing awareness within which telegraphs the most important truth of all. We are not human beings having a spiritual experience. We are Spiritual Beings having a human experience. We are Spirit People! How do Spirit People react when the call comes? Jeremy's last words to me on the phone that day were, "Do you need me?" I answered, "Oh yes. Please come." Jeremy's reply: "I'll be there on the next flight."

Spirit People. They know when to laugh, and they know when to cry. They often have wings and, sometimes, sometimes they fly!

Angels to the Task

Compiled by Jan Rodger

Just as an angel kept Mark alert after his accident and before the paramedics arrived, a number of angels jumped into action to rally prayer for Mark and keep his family and many friends informed about his progress.

Alicia Steinhaus, a friend from Lake Avenue Church in Pasadena, California, set up a Web site for Mark on CaringBridge.com. Various angels in the form of his friends posted updates, enabling "Mark's followers" to rejoice in each step of improvement, large and small, and to pray for him as he faced numerous hurdles. Oh yes, and to be reminded of that inimitable Mark Thallander humor. A few of those postings are highlighted below.

Thursday, August 7, 2003 (posted by Jeremy McElroy)

He [Mark] has eaten about half of his three meals today. He took his first walk down the hall and back this morning and then took a walk around the floor later in the afternoon to view his flowers (some of you may not realize that Mark is allergic to some flowers. Some can stay in the room, but the rest go to other patients and the nurses' stations). He walks with assistance, of course, but thankfully with a bit of spunk and energy that we haven't seen much of thus far. And now as I look to my right, here comes the man of the hour himself, taking his evening walk with the nurse while singing "God Save the Queen"! Typical MT fashion, eh? And no, that is not the medication singing!

Saturday, August 9, 2003 (posted by Jeremy McElroy)

As you all are aware, Mark's birthday is today. We are so happy to report that we threw a very successful bash for him in his room!

About 10 friends from the area surrounded Mark with love, gifts, and cake. He is doing so well right now. His energy is up and he is walking around, already calling the shots! What a delight to see him nearly back to his old self.

Friends and Gary's family surround Mark, the birthday boy, as they celebrate at Maine Medical Center.

More friends, courtesy of Julian Revie, honor Mark and his birthday.

Last night was also very good for him. He kept me up until 2 am! Much time was spent here on the computer reading your greetings to him from the guestbook. He is so excited that so many of you are taking the time to share your love with him. Soon, he should be back on here [the computer] to read the many, many birthday greetings awaiting him.

Monday, August 11, 2003 (posted by John West)
Sunday was a day of new and challenging moments. The first challenge was it was the first day when friend Jeremy was not there. Jeremy had been at Mark's bedside since Monday evening including having a cot set up in the room so Mark would not be alone at night. Jeremy needed to get back to Pittsburgh and his own livelihood, but will be missed greatly by Mark.

Also yesterday Mark's father was removed from the machines that had been supporting his recovery and he passed away. Though not unexpected and in every way he has gone to "receive his crown" (as Mark put it), as you all know this is still a loss of significance. His mom and Wayne [his brother] were there and will be having a funeral service this week. A more enhanced memorial service will take place later after Mark returns - that time to be decided in the future.

Mark has requested that we focus our prayers on the phantom pain feelings he is having. Everything will be normal and then he will suddenly get a jolt of pain that seemingly emanates from a certain part of his missing limb.

Tuesday, August 12, 2003 (posted by John West)
Mark has been transferred. He is now at the New England Rehabilitation Hospital.

He had breakfast and lunch at the Maine Medical Center [MMC] and then transferred in the afternoon to his current location. His projected time stay is seven days. Before he left, the nurses took the drain tubes out and changed his dressing which was then changed again when he arrived at the Rehab Hospital.

The biggest news of the day is, with the help of a physical therapist who guided him through concentrated meditation, Mark was able to actually 'move' the missing arm. Throughout this last week he has been dealing with the physical memory of the arm on his stomach and chest and his fist clenched tightly. He said it took about three and a half hours to accomplish but he eventually was able to move the missing limb from his torso down to his side and unclench the fist. Not only did this relieve him emotionally, he said that it has been a powerful source of the pain. The mind remembers what the body has discarded and this was a GREAT step towards his healing.

Before leaving MMC he had the opportunity to get outside and experience a beautiful Maine night . . . A nurse wheeled him out in a wheelchair where he spent time in the fresh evening air, a first in eight days. Today's transition was smooth and uneventful and allowed him to experience the out of doors a bit more.

He is going into a more aggressive and focused physical therapy now. Having learned how to cut his own meat, open a carton of milk and get the straw in, he is now working on strengthening muscles. Today he climbed one flight of stairs with the railing and a second flight without. He then went down with the same regimen, one with and one without railing. At one point they had him balance on one leg, the goal being one minute. Although he did not reach that goal, he is on his way to it.

So he continues great and steady progress and his spirits are very good.

One final offering for today. The care givers at MMC were very conscious that when Mark came in, there was a good chance he would not survive and were quite impressed by the severity of the accident and the amount of blood he had lost. They said that they really don't know where he got the strength to get through this incident alone, but compounded with the sudden death of his dad they were in awe at how he was handling things. Mark said, "I don't know either," except that he is drawing his strength from the prayers, love and support of so many from around the country and different parts of the world. We do know that God is the primary source, but without his [God's] many tangible and physical hands of friends, family and loved ones, this miracle would not be having such a wonderful ending. Keep the prayers coming; keep the cards coming; keep the love coming. These elements are his [Mark's] life's blood right now that will result in a total and complete recuperation.

Wednesday, August 13, 2003 (posted by Alicia Steinhaus)
The Occupational Therapist put Mark through some focused exercises. One of those exercises was creating and decorating a bulletin board. On one side of the bulletin board are pictures of the car that was in the accident; on another side are cards that he has received; and in the middle is a picture of Merrill Auditorium where the Kotzschmar Series is held. (No, I don't know what or who a Kotzschmar is either. I do know that the divine Joyce Jones will be playing there next week and she is going to stop in and see Mr. Man herself.) The exercise is part of the continuing effort to get Mark to the point where he can function on his own with everyday activities; that is what an Occupational Therapist does.

As the morning progressed he had more visitors. First one from St. Luke's Cathedral and then another who is a board member of the Kotzschmar series. There was much conversation and sharing all the way into and through lunch . . . Then came his time to spend via phone with the funeral of his father.

A cellular phone was used as the conduit and it rested on the pastor's podium. Prior to and after the service Mark did have the opportunity to speak with his mom, which was essential and meaningful for both. The hour long memorial service itself was held in the chapel and opened with a 20 minute prelude from Mark's CD. The officiating pastor, [the] Rev. Eugene Kraft [a long-time friend of the family and a request of Mark's dad], then read from the book of Revelation. This was followed by the Eulogy and Nadine Breneman singing "How Great Thou Art." There were some particularly special moments when letters and thoughts were expressed from the nieces and cousins of Wilfred Lasse Emmanuel Thallander and family. Another moment included an organ tribute of Mark's music which was a medley of "Our Great Savior," "Fairest Lord Jesus" and "All Hail the Power of Jesus' Name." As the congregates were leaving to walk to the grave side burial service they went out to Toccata on "Hymn to Joy" recorded by Mark at the Crystal Cathedral.

The meaningful burial at the graveside was short and highlighted by two members of the Armed Services removing the flag off of the coffin and handing it to Mae Thallander. Then all those in attendance of the celebration of Wilfred's life, sang "The Lord's Prayer" a cappella. As brother Wayne put it, "It was an uplifting celebratory event" which was exactly what the family wanted. I asked Mark how his feelings were with this significant moment and he said with all the phone calls prior, emails and obvious extra effort on behalf of so many he felt "as connected as anyone possibly could." He was very grateful, touched and moved.

This surely would have been enough for any of us, but Mark's day was only half over.

His next hour plus was involved with the Physical Therapist. This consisted of him learning how to get in and out of a normal bed [not hospital bed] without anyone assisting. Also walking outside over bumps and cracks in the pavement, stair climbing and doing all this while maintaining his balance. He also is having elastic bands put in his tennis shoes so he does not have to deal with tying them. Learning how to cut meat, and the basics of everyday things we take for granted, are now his new markers. And, as usual, he tackles these new 'opportunities' earnestly and with gusto.

After this session Gary [DeVaul] arrived with 54 cards, notes and letters!! The timing was good because this is also part of his therapy – learning how to open mail on his own. They both were having a wonderful time when the next guests arrived – the organist and his wife [Albert and Cynthia] from St. Luke's Cathedral. So after a few words and not wanting to stay too sedentary, Mark became a tour guide and took them around to see the facility . . . After dinner Mark headed to the library where he finally had the opportunity to go online. Access had been down for the day and he was eager to read all the new messages that were sent him. When I told him there were well in excess of 6000 hits to his site in only 6 days, he could not help but be impressed . . . neither could I for that matter!!

Tomorrow begins with him and the Occupational Therapist at an 8:00 A.M. cooking class learning how to prepare breakfast.

Thursday, August 14, 2003 (by Mark Thallander, as told to John West)
My day began this morning at 6:30 with a basin of warm water being brought to me and towels so I could bathe. I am now in the process of really learning how to handle my regular daily affairs without any help. Following that I got up, shaved, brushed my teeth, took my morning pills and in time to arrive at the kitchen by 7:45. It was now time for cooking class . . . well, preparation class. The first thing was learning how to cut a bagel and toast it. Then came the challenge of opening a jar of peanut butter and applying it to the toasted bread. This was no small feat since they made sure that the cap was overly tight, which we all have dealt with. I made many attempts, on the counter, against the wall and

finally I got into a corner and by pressing my body against the wall I was able to get enough leverage to open it. Then once I got it open the thick peanut butter was not only at the very bottom, but there was very little of it. This made for another major effort in relinquishing the food from the jar with a knife; all the while the occupational therapist offered no help in the process! Whew, I'm tired just talking about it. After peeling a banana, opening a carton of milk and another of orange juice (all on my own), I was finally was able to 'enjoy' my breakfast.

A word on chocolate ice cream therapy . . .
   I had chocolate ice cream after physical therapy, after occupational therapy, with dinner, after the second "reading of the cards" and just prior to bed. My last words of the evening "Measure by measure, life is a treasure." I guess chocolate really DOES have healing power!!!

Friday, August 15, 2003 (by Mark Thallander, as told to John West)
   The power of Christian memory in regards to Scripture, text and song is such an amazing comfort to me. As I was sitting all alone in the stillness and quiet of the hospital garden today, the words of a choral call to prayer by Don Fontana [former minister of music at the Crystal Cathedral] came to mind:

> *In the stillness of this moment, come to me, come to me;*
> *Let me listen to your wisdom flowing free, flowing free.*
> *In Your nearness speak to me Lord, of Your will and of Your way,*
> *So that glory, power and honor will be Yours in all I do and say.*

Saturday, August 16, 2003 (by Mark Thallander, as told to John West)
   After returning to the facility [the rehab hospital] I was tired but exhilarated with the field trip [my first ride in a car since my accident]. Michael Ross, who was my Certified Nurse's Assistant at Maine Medical Center, came by to do some massage-type physical

therapy. I had another breakthrough. As Michael was massaging my hand, I could feel my non-existent left hand responding. I still have phantom feelings, including the curled, tense and painful third and fifth finger of the left hand. Michael worked on these spots on my right hand and I was able to visualize and feel the relief going into my non-existent digits. This energy relief took a lot of tension out of me, some of which I did not know was still there. I am learning there are a lot of invisible layers that come to light over time when a negative, impacting event of this magnitude has transpired. Layers that must be pulled away in the course of true healing or they hold a person back.

However, the prominent news of the day is that I had my first shower since Sunday, August 3, at 9:00 tonight. The nurse had to prepare the wound very carefully with plastic covering, as it was very important that the area of the amputation did not get wet! I was actually able to drench my body in clean water for the first time in 2 weeks! I was very ready and wonderfully prepared to go to bed after a very positive, but exhausting day.

Tuesday, August 19, 2003 (by Mark Thallander, as told to Jeremy McElroy)
Today is Tuesday, August 19, 2003, the day I will finally be released from in-patient care. After 15 days, a half month, I will be able to sleep away from the hospital and enjoy the comforts of a home; comforts that each of us can often take for granted. After some morning "routines" of meals and therapy, my day continued to be full. This evening, I will be attending the concert of my dear friend Joyce Jones here in Portland, Maine. Afterwards will be the 40 minute drive south to Gary's home in Ogunquit, Maine. The weather is absolutely perfect and rivals even the best moments in Southern California! I know that my first day out will prove to be very therapeutic . . . I was so happy to be able to focus my energies on some recreation and relaxation today too, a much deserved break from the relentless path of adjustment I have embarked upon.

Today I experienced minimal pain. I talked with Jeremy, and he said he heard joy in my voice today! The support and prayers of so many, many people continue to be actualized in my life. Please continue to lift me up in prayer and specifically pray for pain management.

Wednesday, August 20, 2003 (by Mark Thallander, as told to Jeremy McElroy)

Today was my first full day out of the hospital and I indulged myself completely – maybe a little TOO completely. I slept in and arose at 10:45; the longest time and opportunity I've had to sleep. Gary and John West (who is visiting for a day and a half) and I went to Amore Breakfast for a wonderful meal of fancy French toast with berries, whipped cream and REAL maple syrup. It was delicious. Following that full bodied meal we took an hour's walk along Marginal Way (often singing at the top of our lungs) which ended up in a lovely cove called Perkins Cove. It was beautiful but it was also hot – about 91 degrees. It was time to stop for refreshment and that refreshment was chocolate and vanilla soft ice cream swirl.

Mark is joined by Phil DeVaul (left), Gary DeVaul, and Leanne Cusimano, owner of Amore Breakfast.

Mark poses outside Amore Breakfast.

After that we came home and took a few minutes to recuperate. Then it was off to the downtown area of Ogunquit where we indulged in the afternoon sunshine as well as a walk in and out of the quaint shops. From there we took a little excursion down the Coast of Rt. 1, stopping at scenic areas along the way and ending up in Portsmouth where I had the opportunity to FINALLY get my glasses fixed. They had been damaged in the auto accident and had been causing problems. On the way back we took a side trip to actually see the place where the accident happened. It was a sobering moment to see the place where the accident took place. As we approached, my missing hand started to have a phantom reaction and tense up. John and Gary got out of the car and walked around the site. Although no exact conclusions could be made, it was a defining moment in understanding what possibly happened the evening of August 3rd.

Saturday, August 23, 2003 (posted by Jeremy McElroy)

Mark is very excited about the next step of his rehabilitation treatment. He will go to the York Hospital in York, Maine where he is with a very talented Physical Therapist [Stephán]. His appointments are for 3 times a week for the next 2 weeks. He also has an appointment in Portland this coming Monday to have the staples in his shoulder looked at and hopefully removed. I saw the shoulder during my week with Mark and I must say that I was amazed. It looks so good. We need to be very grateful that God allowed such a fine plastic surgeon to care for him.

As we have mentioned before there are a myriad of cards that Mark has received. He counts over 600 now. During both hospital stays, Mark had most of his cards read to him by one of us. Now, he has been able to go back and read them for himself. He has spent the last two days reading each and every one. He has a huge basket full of all the cards that you have sent. It is another valuable and effective tool of encouragement for him.

One other fun sight is the host of butlers he has at his feet. Of course, they don't actually do anything. They don't fetch a glass of water or prepare an Epsom salt soak for his feet. They don't even look up when he calls (which I hope he doesn't do much of!). No, the butlers are a group of 10 stuffed monkeys [see photo on page 69]! If any of you know Julian Revie, you will understand the humor of this fun-loving, smiling Canadian. Julian serves as the organist for Lake Avenue Church in Pasadena, CA. He is fortunate to have a friend who is also in Ogunquit this summer. Together, the two of them arranged the gift of the ten little butlers! Mark was very instrumental in Julian being introduced to Lake Ave Church. One source of entertainment for all is Gary's Springer Spaniel, Casey. He wasn't so thrilled about the monkeys.

One very significant activity of today was Mark watching the video of his father's funeral. The house was quiet and empty and Mark had the time to himself. It was important that he be able to do this, especially now that he is feeling more energetic and can focus his mind better. He spoke with his mother afterwards who said she has received many, many cards of support and encouragement as well. She is very appreciative to each of you who have kept her and Mark's brother Wayne in your prayers over the past couple weeks.

Monday, August 25, 2003 (posted by Jeremy McElroy)

One major area of concern that all of us have had is that regarding the future of Mark's music making and worship leading. We are delighted to let you know that at least 2 pieces of music for Mark are already being composed. His dear friend Joyce Jones, who played in Portland last week, is working on a hymn suite to be specifically for 1 right hand and 2 feet.

To motivate Mark and prepare him for it, Joyce has provided a mentor organist: a one armed doll! Mark is just so happy about it. It even has an organist's robe that hangs down more in the back than in the front so as not to disturb the pedaling!

Another friend is Charles Callahan, avid composer and arranger of organ literature. Several pieces that Mark and I have played were arranged by him. One of his areas of specialty is writing for organ duo, or as Mark entitled our June [2003] noon day recital at the Cathedral of Our Lady of the Angels in Los Angeles, "Two Organists, One Bench!" Dr. Callahan sent Mark a card recently and in it, told of his new piece for the two of us to play for 3 hands, 4 feet, plus he is composing a piece for Mark called "Fanfare of Hope." Open your calendars, all ye church music ministers, for the Mark Thallander and Friends organ tour train should be steaming into your town soon!

Wednesday, August 27, 2003 (by Mark Thallander, as told to Jeremy McElroy)

From the East and the West we came to study at Central Bible College in Springfield, Missouri. When I was a freshman, the *Revivaltime* organist was Judy Casso from New York! Two dear friends of ours from those CBC days, Sandy Ford and Judy Hanlon, decided there should be a special reunion in Ogunquit. So, the three of them came to see me! We had a terrific dinner last night. I am told we tore up the town! How could we not have been noticed? The four of us singing old gospels songs as we strolled through the quaint little village!

This morning we feasted at our favorite place in Ogunquit: Amore Breakfast. After breakfast we took a walk on the pathway along the shore and overlooking the water called the Marginal Way. The Marginal Way leads to Perkins Cove, a charming area of shops, galleries, and of course, chocolate ice cream! Ah, it's healing at its finest, isn't it? Prayer, chocolate, prayer, chocolate! Another treat from Perkins Cove was seeing the organist, Ann-Marie Johnson, from the Ogunquit Baptist Church.

Enjoying a special reunion at Amore Breakfast are Central Bible College friends (l-r) Sandy Ford, Mark, Judy Hanlon, and Judy (nee Casso) DiGiandomenico.

Yesterday's visit to the doctor in Portland was very good. The doctor removed all of the staples from my shoulder and said that the skin is healing up very nicely. As I was leaving the office, yet another person said hello to me. It was Julie Downing, the wife of Larry Downing, the choir director at the Ogunquit Baptist Church! Julie works for one of the surgeons who was at my side the night of the accident. It's a small world, after all!

Monday, September 15, 2003 (posted by John West)

He was in and out like a flash flood, only it was more than that – he was washing us with the presence of his return.

Mark passed through Pasadena on Saturday on his way to a family reunion in Stockton, Sunday through Wednesday. He slept well in his own bed for the first time in many months and had the opportunity to be in his own home.

[On Sunday, cousins] Diane, Tony and Aunt Eva picked Mark up at the Sacramento airport and took him to Stockton to see his mom and brother Wayne; quite an emotional reunion as you can imagine. Then off to a dinner at Aunt Dodie's to see North Dakota relatives Jayne and Lorraine. Today [Monday] he has a meeting with Nadine Breneman and cousin Diane to work on details for the memorial celebration reception [for his father], and Tuesday night he'll have dinner with some Stockton friends. Then Wednesday it's back to Pasadena for him, and Thursday he gives his first lesson!! This will be the start of his new life which will include more doctors' appointments, more therapy and eventually a new arm!

Mark visits with his mother and his brother, Wayne, during his first time back in Stockton, California, after his accident.

Mark is flanked by (l-r) cousins Lorraine, Diane, and Joyce and his brother, Wayne.

Cousins Diane and Joyce and his brother, Wayne, join Mark in celebrating his return to Stockton.

One last anecdote. At dinner with Paul [Bandy, Mark's neighbor and apartment manager who now serves as chair of the Mark A. Thallander Trust], Mark told a story of his experience when he accidentally was over medicated with morphine. He could see himself drifting away in that renowned tunnel of light, on his "way to Heaven." But there were voices that kept yelling at him. "Mark, you are in a hospital," "Mark, this is Dr. so and so," "Mark, keep breathing." He eventually came back to his hospital room to the faces of Gary and the hospital staff. Mark commented how twice he has almost died, and twice the angels brought him back. He KNOWS with an eagerness of voice and without a shadow of doubt that God has something for him to do. All of us are part of that!

Welcome Home, you good and faithful servant. We await our new journey with you!

Body and Blood

by Gary DeVaul

It's a cool Sunday morning with a flood of sunshine. All across Maine there are tourists packing up, preparing to return home after a sometimes wet, but mostly sunny, summer holiday. Labor Day weekend is like that, you know. It's back to school, back to work, back to another fall.

As I write this, Mark is walking some ten minutes to the Baptist church in the village. I played hooky to capture a little piece of peace because, if you know Mark, you know that when he's around, things are poppin'! Phones are ringing, dates are being made, visitors seem nonstop, and calendars are being filled. It's time for this painkiller, or that medicine. And then there's the "Hey, Gary! Would you button this for me?" What a character he is. What a privilege to be part of his life these past almost thirty years. And that's why I'm writing. Mark's not with you physically; he's with me. Many of you understand that we are all one, one in the Spirit, of course, but it's even more tangible than that. We are one in the flesh as well. And you have a right to know how your brother is doing.

All across the Ogunquit shire, from the lobster pound to the village square, there are large and small churches and meeting houses. This morning as I write to you, the Host is being lifted up in every village and town. The litany of words is the same everywhere, over every altar, upon countless Communion tables, "This is My body, this is My blood." And when our blessed Lord uttered those words, He, too, understood the physical as well as spiritual connection that unites us all – not just as persons, but as part of His Father's creation. Oh, Jesus probably didn't understand the astonishing science of DNA and the fact that the trees and grass and you and me are all made of the same carbon-based stuff. Then again, maybe He did. He is all-knowing. He knew that if He were lifted up on the broad beam of the cross, we, too, would be lifted with Him. He knew that in a thousand different ways His suffering and resurrection were our suffering and resurrection. He was – and is – aware of the fact that we are as connected to one another physically as we are spiritually. "This is My body, this is My blood" is not just something that He said, or the proverbial "they" say. It's what we say, you and I as we live together.

Today as I watched Mark cross the lawn, pass the garage, walk under the flag and down the driveway to church, I felt a pang of guilt for not accompanying him. Yet I knew where he was going, what he was doing, who he would meet along the way. In a sense I was with him, and so were you, because he is part of us - and we him.

The German philosopher Arthur Schopenhauer once told the story of a small boy in Berlin at the turn of the century who broke from his mother and ran out into the bustling avenue in front of a carriage drawn by four horses. An old man saw the boy in harm's way and instinctively jumped in front of the horses, knocking the boy to safety and losing his legs in the effort. It was an awful, bloody mess. When questioned, the old man replied, "I didn't have time to think of the consequences. I saw the boy and I jumped." That was a physical reaction to our spiritual connectedness. That was Jesus jumping for us, for you and me, and for the boy. "This is My body, this is My blood." There is no other appropriate response. The old man lost his legs and saved the boy. In doing so, he saved a bit of each of us that day.

This is not something that the proverbial "they" did, or even "he" did. This is something that a man did. A real flesh-and-blood man. It is played out many times on this planet, in our world, but we forget to apply it to ourselves. When we hear, or say, the formula instituted by Jesus, "This is My body, this is My blood, do this in remembrance of Me," it has a tendency to be too familiar. The words somehow lose their meaning. It becomes like the "they" we often allude to in our conversations. "They" will take care of it, or "they" will take care of him or her. But there is no "they" here, only us. We must do it. We must accept the responsibility for one of our own. When we do, when we save our brother or sister, we save a part of ourselves as well. It was Jesus who said, "I and the Father are one" (John 10:30). And it was Jesus who referred to Himself as our Brother. The connection was real to Him, and through our daily acts of redemption for one another, the words become flesh and Jesus lives again and again.

It's important that I report that Mark is doing well, both physically and mentally. It's been amazing to watch his body respond. Every cell knows what to do in coordination with every other cell. He's building new blood, digesting food, fighting off infection, controlling his temperature, breathing, eating, dressing, thinking, talking, laughing, and, yes, crying. What a miracle the human creation is! Every molecule, every subatomic particle, every neutron, every electron making up every atom knows exactly what to do in order to live and heal and respond to every other atom and to Mark's needs. God's hand is in every bit of it, and it's marvelous to our eyes. And, of course, we see this recovery and we can say, "This is my body, this is my blood," because it is. The sympathy we feel for one another at a time like this is the emotional response to the spiritual reality that we, too, are part of one another and that we, too, are the body of Christ. The spiritual body of Christ must react as do the very cells of our physical bodies.

The body of Christ, of which you and I are a part, must engage in a coordinated response as well. The Mark A. Thallander Trust has been established by friends for Mark's support through this difficult time. He has some physical pain, but it's not nearly what it once was. Now he has to contend with the very real concerns of how to support himself, how to pay the bills, when he leaves the haven of Ogunquit. He never complains but, I must say, I see it in his face. He is a hero, but heroes know the face of fear and uncertainty as we all do. "Father, if you are willing, remove this cup from Me; yet not My will, but Yours be done" (Luke 22:42).

Some time ago Mark asked me to go to the junkyard where the

Toyota 4Runner that he was driving the night of the accident was impounded. He wanted me to see if I could retrieve CD recordings of the Twentieth Anniversary Concert of the Hazel Wright Organ at the Crystal Cathedral. Mark wanted to give the CDs to the nurses at the hospital as a "thank you" for all that they had done for him. Mark's contributions to the concert, recorded on the CD, were the first and last pieces played. The finale was the marvelous old warhorse that is used at the close of many a worship service. It is the thundering, rapturous Widor Toccata, and Mark played it perfectly to a standing ovation.

Well, I found the CDs lying on the back floor of the Toyota literally covered with blood and glass. Mark lost five units of blood in that vehicle the night of the crash, and you can imagine the remnants of the carnage. I lifted the CDs from the wreckage and took them home. As I washed them, I could not help but see the pink water swirling down the sink and think of my best buddy. The words kept pounding through my brain, "This is **my** body, this is **my** blood." I don't think I'll ever hear those words of consecration in quite the same way again. The connection is too real and the responsibility of love too great. We must respond.

There ain't no *they*, folks. Just you, and me, and Jesus.

Gary's Toyota 4Runner at the junkyard

Choosing Life

by Gary DeVaul

Mark was in a conversation with a friend when the friend asked a simple question that all of us have asked through the aftermath of his accident. "Mark, how do you remain so positive? Your attitude is remarkable; your recovery is amazing to me." In and out of formal ministry I've heard this question asked of others, and of course like all of you, I've asked it myself. The answer to the question can be of great importance to all of us in our daily lives, in our struggles great and small.

When I was studying at Fuller Theological Seminary in Pasadena, California, the late Dr. Paul Jewett preached a sermon on 2 Corinthians 4:7-12: "But we have this treasure in earthen vessels, so that the surpassing greatness of the power will be of God and not from ourselves; we are afflicted in every way, but not crushed; perplexed, but not despairing; persecuted, but not forsaken; struck down, but not destroyed; always carrying about in the body the dying of Jesus, so that the life of Jesus also may be manifested in our body. For we who live are constantly being delivered over to death for Jesus' sake, so that the life of Jesus also may be manifested in our mortal flesh. So death works in us, but life in you."

A few years later my mentor, Dr. Raymond Beckering at Garden Grove Community Church, chose to preach on that same passage at my ordination. He entitled his sermon "Cracked Pots." Boy, was he ever right on!

Ray said, "Earthen vessels — well, that's us, isn't it?" Earthen vessels crack sooner or later, don't they? And, of course, when they do, that which they contain comes pouring out. That's what we mean when we see people being tested and we say, "Now we'll see what they're made of." And, of course, we do . . . if we pay attention.

On one occasion in the hospital, the machine that was dispensing Mark's pain medication ceased to function. It was supposed to beep when that happened, but for some reason the contraption failed to beep and Mark got behind the pain curve. The medication they were giving him exits your body very rapidly, and it takes some time before the new dose can catch up to the pain. That's what it means to be behind the pain curve.

Because of the brutality of Mark's accident and injury, his left arm was pulled off at the shoulder rather than being cleanly severed. In the process the nerves and vascular system were shredded, and the resulting pain in recovery was severe. As the painkiller was ebbing and the pain was increasing, Mark asked me to readjust his pillows. I did, but it didn't help. Soon the veins in his forehead were bulging, and his eyes were filling with tears. I headed for the nurses' station, only to be told to wait a minute while the nurse finished her telephone call – something about putting "a leg of lamb in the oven." Well, that didn't go over very well, and my legendary impatience flared! Suffice it to say, the nurse was there in a jiffy. She fixed the machine and dispensed the pain medication, and we waited what seemed an eternity for the medication to kick in.

The pain increased for awhile, but in his suffering Mark didn't curse or carry on. He just asked to hold my hand, and we both prayed. Now that's what Mark is made of. There, through the cracks in the earthen vessel, I could see the "transcendent power of God" doing what the transcendent power does best – it transcends! It asked only for the hand of a friend, and it gracefully transcended the pain and agony until the medicine kicked in.

Oh, by the way, I apologized to the nurse. She replied, "Honey, I've been dealing with idiots all my life. Don't worry about it." She knew a cracked pot when she saw one.

We learned about machines that day. We watched them carefully from then on. But we also learned about being struck down without being destroyed. The transcendent power never imposes itself upon us. But if we choose to tap into it, it never fails us either. It is the choosing that is important. The power is activated by our prayerful choice. "I have set before you life and death, the blessing and the curse. So chose life" (Deut. 30:19b). This is part of what the apostle Paul meant when he said, "Always carrying about in the body the dying of Jesus, so that the life of Jesus also may be manifested in our body" (2 Cor. 4:10). We often suffer as Jesus suffered, but if we choose as He chose, there is resurrection as well.

When asked by our friend how he manages to be cheerful and have such a positive attitude, Mark simply replied, "What's the alternative? We can choose to go up, or we can allow the gravity of the situation to take us down." Mark chose life. Sometimes that's not easy.

Often when confronted with obstacles as challenging as losing an arm, good manners and cultural norms have to be put aside in order to function, and a well-honed sense of humor is important.

One evening we went to the Five-O Shore Road restaurant in the village. Mark ordered his favorite entrée, a hamburger. Usually, if I'm nearby, I will remember to cut his food. This time I forgot, and here was this huge hamburger wiggling and squiggling, not wanting to be lifted with one hand. I looked up from my meal to see that Mark had stuck his fork into the burger and, with his face just a few inches from his food, was holding the handle of the fork with his teeth, while cutting the all-American meal with a knife in his right hand! Not a pretty sight, you say? Well, of course, I was embarrassed for him, and I moved quickly to cut the thing in half. "What are you doing?" I asked Mark. He spit out the fork and replied, "I'm trying to kill it before I eat it." The good people sitting next to us had been eavesdropping. They could see that Mark was struggling with one arm, and they were captivated by sympathy. Upon hearing his declaration of burgercide, they were disarmed and erupted in laughter.

Attitude has to do with how we live moment by moment, without struggling to choose our reaction incident by incident. Through years of prayerfully working on his attitude, Mark has learned to live moment by moment, choosing life over death. And the transcendent power shows forth, and we are amazed. By the way, humor is a by-product of God's grace, an absolutely essential element in choosing to choose life.

Now don't get me wrong. Canonizing Mark might please him, but I doubt it. He's still as full of stuffing as a Christmas turkey! He eats way too much ice cream. His cell phone has become an appendage of his ear. He's addicted to his computer, and his playful sense of humor borders on the mischievous at times. And, of course, living with someone who always chooses life can be a real pain in the neck. But then we're all cracked pots, aren't we?

By the way, when your days get sticky, just visualize our buddy killing that hamburger with a fork in his mouth. The transcendent power will laugh, and so will you! Cracked pots every one . . .

The Questions

by Gary DeVaul

Hurricane Isabel did her thing the other day. Way up here in Maine we received just the edge of her wrath, lots of rain. I took a trip to the crash site during one of her more lavish downpours. As the fringe of her gray robe brushed across York County, Maine, I found that indeed the place where the 4Runner lost traction had ample water to hydroplane. The tire marks that indicated where the SUV left the road, crossed the grass, and crashed into the guardrail were grown over as a result of nature's healing.

As I write this, I know that the little pieces of plastic tape the nurse put over Mark's scars when he removed the staples are dissolving and falling away, as they are meant to do. Soon the scars will fade and blend and Mark's shoulder will not be hard to look at. Oh, there's still a small remnant of glass swept into a pile at the base of one of the pillars that supports the guardrail, but even that's diminishing. The signs of the 4Runner's green paint are difficult to find. Pretty soon most of the physical indications of the wreck that changed Mark's life will have fled the scene of the crime. But there will still be questions. And the questions are more important than the answers.

There are questions regarding the physical aspects of the accident. Why would the State of Maine allow the drainage to be so inadequate at this important and dangerous turn in the road? Why would brand new Michelin tires, engineered for snow and rain, lose their grip? The accident report and diagram are before me as I write. The vehicle slid sideways into the guardrail. Yet the whole frame and steal cage protecting the driver, door and all, were shoved into the driver's seat, moving the seat over until it rested up against the gearshift, bending the steering wheel, bowing the dashboard into a half moon, and popping out the speedometer, leaving it perched on the post of the steering wheel. How could the impact be so great as to break most of the windows, tossing the car over the rail into oncoming traffic? What could cause the vehicle to land with such force that it broke the rear axle, sending the right rear wheel into orbit? How could a seat belt, which is made to protect, tear off someone's arm, severing it in three different places? The belt was cut in the attempt to retrieve the driver, but it was still fastened. I saw the beltless latch engaged with my own eyes! And finally, how could most of the windows, including the sunroof and windshield, shatter without leaving a mark, not one cut on the driver, save his severed left arm?

Even if Mark was driving too fast for the weather conditions, the police said that he was not exceeding the posted speed limit. There are loads of questions regarding the physical aspects of the crash. And then there is the really difficult spiritual question that tramps across every mind and trumps all the other questions. The question no one wants to ask.

This is the question that is more important than the answer!

But we don't feel at all comfortable asking it. And it's because we don't want to struggle with it that we must. Do the possibilities frighten us? Or are we too lazy to work, and think, and pray, and meditate on it? Maybe it's just easier to chalk it up to "God's will" and hustle back to some safe place in our heads.

Remember, God is revealing Himself to us every day. We see His face in Scripture, in nature, in science, in the world around us, as well as in the accidents that befall us. His natural, continuous revelation didn't stop with the invention of the printing press. His language is not limited to sixteenth-century syntax or the King James Version of the Bible. All indications are that He is alive and well and completely engaged in our universe and in our very lives! So the question is this . . .

Why did God allow this to happen?

Well, there are all kinds of answers. But know this – I don't pretend to have the solution. Nevertheless, all followers of Jesus Christ have the right – indeed obligation – to ask the question. We need to probe in prayer and scour the Scriptures to read the thoughts of others who also work and struggle with this question. Why? Because it's in the asking, in questioning, in the engagement of the intellectual powers that He gave us that God is blessed. Why? Because it is in this way that we get to know Him better. It's in struggle and strife that spiritual growth takes place. That's why the questions are more important than the answers. We want our children to question, to learn and grow, and to hound us for answers. Being a follower of Jesus doesn't mean we go merrily on our passive ways, accepting all that happens to others and us without storming the gates of heaven. To say "Well, I'll have plenty of questions to ask when I get to heaven" is to imply that God is not speaking to us today.

We have a big God. Divinity is not insulted by inquiry. He doesn't get His feelings hurt because we want to understand. He's not angered by our honest concerns. He's the God of the universe. He can handle it.

Years ago I was helping a Lutheran minister teach a Pastor's Class of people who wished to join the church. A man asked an age-old question. "Pastor," he queried, "why does God let some people go to hell?" And the minister replied, "That's not the right question to ask." Then he went on to answer a related question that he could handle with ease and confidence. I almost fell out of my chair. After the class I went to the minister and said, "How dare you tell that man that he was asking the wrong question? How dare you imply that you know the right question? Is it too difficult to say, 'I don't know the answer, but let's talk about it together'?" Needless to say, I was never invited to help him teach the Pastor's Class again.

Every one of us has the right to ask God why this horrible accident happened to Mark. And every one of us also needs to remember that Mark was not cut, nor was he bruised, nor blinded, nor killed. Angels again? You bet.

If we don't get the answers that we pray for and we get angry with God and lie on the floor of the temple and bang our fists on the altar . . . if we holler at God, like David did when he was losing his baby son . . . don't worry about it. God can handle it. He understands our pain, our anger, and our frustration. Our God is no sissy. We will get our answers. Be patient. Be persistent. They will come. Time will bring a fresh flush of perspective. When God hears our prayers and senses our frustration, it means something to Him. I'll bet that He feels just as I do when my boys demand answers of me. It makes Him proud of His children, proud that they care about their brothers and sisters, proud that they are concerned about justice, proud that they're not intellectually lazy, proud that they feel they have a close enough relationship to ask the hard questions.

Do you think Mark hasn't asked the question? Well, he has. Something else I'll tell you about Mark. He knows that his heavenly Father loves him. He knows that he was not alone in the vehicle that night. He knows that God has called him by name, and that neither all the waves in the world, nor all the fires of fear, nor all the accidents conceivable can amputate the Spirit that lives within him. He knows that God never promised life would be fair. But he also knows that, through the act on the cross, Jesus proved that He is with us. With us and for us always, even unto the ends of the earth, and beyond!

When I left the crash site, I turned on the CD player in my car. Guess who was playing? I had forgotten that Mark had left the recording of the Twentieth Anniversary Concert of the Hazel Wright Organ at the Crystal Cathedral in the player before he went to California. Many of our great friends performed in that concert. Every one of them is a genius in his own right. Frederick Swann, Richard Unfried, J. Christopher Pardini. And who did they choose to open and close the concert? Mark Thallander, of course! What an honor! Although he would never claim to be in their league, he rose to the occasion.

Listening again to Mark play his arrangement of Toccata on "Hymn to Joy," I was reminded of something one of those men taught me thirty years ago when I was a young man in ministry at Garden Grove Community Church.

As a music lover, I used to schedule my breaks so I could listen to Richard Unfried practice for the Sunday services. I'm sure I was a pest, but he never let on. One day Richard was registering the organ for a great piece that everyone knew. It was the Bach Toccata and Fugue in D Minor. He called it the "old warhorse," and he wanted to make it a unique performance and register the new Ruffatti organ a bit differently. In the process, I had the opportunity to hear all kinds of pipes make all kinds of sounds. I heard harsh biting reeds, booming trumpets, and all kinds of stuff that alone might not necessarily be kind to one's ear. Then Richard put them all together, and I was stunned! I'd never heard such wonderful sounds in my life. How many times have you watched your mother cook a meal and then crinkled up your nose at the fixin's, asking "Do you have to put *that* in there?" Looking back, how many meals did she prepare that you really didn't like?

Well, I don't know half of the answers, but this I know. Richard Unfried didn't make those pipes. He took what he had to work with and made music with it. And it was marvelous to the ear and to the soul. God didn't make that car crash. But He did send angels to gather up the remnants, like so many leftover pieces of bread at Galilee. And from the leftovers of Mark's life, the world will be fed and blessed and better for it. As we remain faithful to God and our questions, we will grow. The answers will unfold in time and space before us. And the angels? Oh, they'll continue to thoughtfully thrive in the tension between questions and answers. They will learn and grow in their faith, and they will support Mark's recovery and ministry. Won't you, angels all?

Pallets

by Gary DeVaul

Looking at pictures of the green 4Runner, one realizes that the only way to pull Mark from the wreckage was through the sunroof. It must have been like lifting him from the grave. The scene is reminiscent of the wonderful story of the paralytic in Mark 2:1-12. Only in the gospel account the problem was reversed. They couldn't get the man in to see Jesus, so they lowered him through the roof!

Can you imagine? The word was out that Jesus was at home resting. He was back in Capernaum. He was hopefully taking a break. Rarely was Jesus spoken of as having a home. And we know little of the details regarding this one. We don't know whose name was on the deed, or if there even was one. But we do know Mark's gospel refers to it as home, and we do know how the homes were built in Capernaum because many of them still exist today.

The houses were made of stone and mud and usually had packed dirt floors. The rafters stretched across the span of the house. The space between the rafters was filled with rushes and mud and anything people could find. Grass grew abundantly on the roof!

Well, it doesn't sound like Jesus got much rest at home. The place was filled with people. There were undoubtedly sick people, wounded people, paralyzed people, and blind people. And then there were the scribes, the media of the day, always ready to give Jesus bad press. Not exactly a day to kick back and watch the game.

We forget sometimes that Jesus was known as Rabbi, or Teacher. And that's exactly what He was doing that day at home in Capernaum. He was teaching, when all of sudden some yahoo started digging through the ceiling. Can you imagine what Jesus and His disciples were thinking? All this grass and dirt started falling into the room! Not a Good Housekeeping day, you say? Well, there was a lot more going on than met the eye. And you can count on Jesus' sense of awareness to capture the moment.

There was a man outside on a pallet. A paralytic. He couldn't move. He wanted to see and hear Jesus teach, but he was frozen to his pallet. He couldn't get to Jesus himself, so he enlisted four friends to help him. They were the angels that do the heavy lifting. Now they got this guy on the roof and started digging a hole in the grass on top of the house. Forget the commotion that this must have been causing below. Picture the house and see the imagery.

The grass roof represents the place of burial. The hole in the roof is the grave. Paralyzed and helpless as if dead, the man was being lowered into the pit. And whom did he find waiting for him in the place of death? The Author of Life.

The symbolism is powerful, and Jesus Himself confirmed it. If this were just about healing, the man would have been healed first. But it wasn't. The physical healing was secondary; the paralysis was a symptom of a spiritual problem. Spiritual life verses spiritual death was at issue here, and Jesus went to the heart of the matter and forgave the man his sins. When the spirit is healed, life is restored and the tomb becomes the womb.

Now, the skeptical scribes in the room with Jesus didn't get it. They got hung up on the fact that Jesus was forgiving sins. They failed to see the relationship between life, death, and the resurrection that pertains to spirit. The scribes were sure that Jesus was trying to claim some kind of Divine authority that was not rightly His in their minds. They thought, well, now we've got Him – it's heresy! Well, they were wrong. He was not making such claims. He was deliberately referring to Himself as the Son of Man. Interestingly enough, this is the only time in Mark's gospel that Jesus referred to Himself as the Son of Man in relationship to the forgiveness of sins. He purposely did this in order to derail the scribes' attempt to capture Him in a theological conundrum and to get them back on track. He was saying, "Hey, guys, let's not play games here. The man's spirit is at the heart of the issue."

Well, the scribes missed the point. The media often do because they usually have their own agendas. So Jesus said, "Listen up! The Holy Spirit has transformed. The man is forgiven. Life is restored. Now the pallet has lost its power and the man is healed. You want proof of that? You there! Get up! Pick up your pallet and go home." The man did just that, and of course they were all amazed.

In this gospel story, the pallet and paralysis are symbolic of the spiritual nature of the problem. The paralysis, sickness, or whatever ails, becomes symptomatic. Jesus did not tell the man to just rise and go home. He did not tell the man to rise and clean up the mess he made in His living room. He told him to get up, take that which had bore him, and bear it! Now that he's spiritually fit, he can master the problem and carry the pallet.

By telling him to take it home, Jesus was instructing the man to make his problem his own. Jesus knew that the pallet would give birth to possibilities and become the springboard to something greater. This is how tombs become wombs! Mark Thallander will tell you that it is true. He's seen the tomb. And because you've helped do the heavy lifting, the loss of his arm will, through its identification with the Spirit, become a blessing rather than a curse.

Last week Mark scheduled time to play the pipe organ at Glendale Presbyterian Church. He wasn't exactly sure how it would work, with one hand and two feet. But that was his problem, and he was going to master it. He prayed and worked, rearranged, and practiced. At the end of his time at the organ, he met a woman who was cleaning the sanctuary. She had been praying for him every day since his accident, helping to lift him onto the roof.

She feared that he would never play again and was worried about how he would handle the loss of his vocation, as well as his arm. At the end of his practice time, she greeted him. It was an emotional moment. She said that she would never have thought it possible. She couldn't tell the difference in his playing.

Looking through the jagged hole in the top of the green 4Runner, mingled with dirt, and blood, and grass, Jesus found Mark bleeding to death, strapped in the seat, his own grave. One hand was gone; yet another appeared through the roof. There was a scar on its palm. "Come on, Mark," the kind voice said. "Don't cry. No, no, we'll not mix tears with blood tonight, for I have shed enough for both of us. I know My own Spirit when I see it. Take My hand, and we're out of here. We have music to make. Your left hand is no phantom; it is Mine."

They left together that night in the dark, through the wind and the rain. If you look with your heart, you will see them both. Mark carried off through the tall, wet grass in the arms of Jesus. If you listen with your soul, you will hear the fastidious Thallander say, "Oh, wow! I sure made a mess back there." And then His voice, "Don't worry about it, buddy. Remember, I'm a carpenter. I'll fix the roof, and we'll get those four angels to do the heavy lifting and clean up the mess in the living room."

And you will, won't you? Clean up the mess, I mean?

The Changeling

by Gary DeVaul

A Changeling is an impish child, deftly put in the place of another by fairies in folk tales. The Changeling for some represents the Trickster, the one who throws us curves in life. The Changeling is ambivalent. It cares for neither good nor evil; it just loves to watch us squirm. Ancient mythology teaches us that the Changeling is only stymied when we take its curve ball and hit a home run with it. Even then, the Changeling is relentless. It never stops pitching; it has an inevitable quality.

Mark and I have a good friend here in Ogunquit, Maine. He's an interesting man, and he drives antique cars. Our friend doesn't like change, and he's pretty vociferous about it. The Changeling loves to watch him squirm. Our friend likes the old dirt road that leads up to his beautiful house overlooking Ogunquit and the sea beyond. But he is faced with a dilemma. Change for the road is just around the corner. Hurricane Isabel shed her angry tears on us and washed the road out again. Our friend is frustrated now. He has to pave the road, and he resents the change. He's not alone. We've all experienced the frustration of change and the challenges it brings.

For Mark, change came in a matter of seconds; seconds that will stretch into years; seconds that will reach into every mundane and monumental moment of his life; seconds that have changed, on a subterranean level, his life, my life, and some of yours as well. After all, are not our lives an accumulation of seconds, each one transformed by voluntary or involuntary change? There are two questions that bubble to the surface. Are we going to react to the changes in our lives with anger, fear, and frustration? Or are we going to recognize these mutations as watershed, crossroad experiences and allow the Holy Spirit to enable us to transform pain into personal progress? It's true that every problem offers us possibilities for progress. Within every prospective problem is the inherent opportunity for spiritual growth and physical and financial progress, just to name a few. But the one thing we can take to the bank with us is this: *Change is inevitable. Progress is not. Progress is up to you and me.*

When confronted by spectacularly profound change, it is usually time to rethink who we are and what we're doing. The accident of August 3, 2003, was Mark's personal equivalent of our nation's September 11, 2001. Nine-Eleven forced us all to sort and sift our national consciousness and, in a very real sense, redefined who we are. Every day that we turned on the television and saw the newscasts, we were confronted with the permanence and the surreal loss of those beautiful buildings and the lives they carried within. No matter how many times we turned the television off and on again, the loss would not go away. The only thing permanent about change is its inevitability. Change is inevitable.

Because we didn't want Mark to fall behind the pain curve again, it was my job to see to it that he didn't oversleep and wasn't late in taking his medicine. Every morning I would begin my day by awakening him and would see the bandages and the arm that was not there. And every morning I would see the look on his face as he awoke to the knowledge that it was real, that it was gone . . . that the change was permanent. Where did he go with the painful realization of the moment? Where did our nation go immediately after 9/11? Our nation gathered at the National Cathedral in Washington, D.C. Mark went to the temple within. He would close his eyes and go to the sacred center within, find grace, and then take his medicine. He did not squirm and fight the Changeling. He embraced the challenge. Every morning the Changeling's curve ball was pitched, and every morning Mark managed to reach within and hit a home run. Well, at least a base hit.

In John 8:1-11, Jesus sets the example for us regarding how we are to behave in the face of the Changeling's tricky challenges. Jesus the Rabbi was teaching in the temple. In the Gospels, when Jesus is referred to as Rabbi or Teacher, it is a call for us to listen up! For the Teacher is about to teach us something vital to our personal spiritual progress.

A gang of scribes and Pharisees, the equivalent of our media and lawyers/politicians, approached Jesus with a woman in tow. They had been waiting for the opportunity to catch Jesus in the temple in front of His students and embarrass Him. The whole deal was a setup. So they undoubtedly entrapped the woman and brought her to Him. It's an important moment. The challenge of the Changeling was in the air. The woman's life hung in the balance. And remember, they could bring charges against Jesus if He answered incorrectly.

The accusers said, "Look here, Rabbi. We caught this woman in the very act of adultery. We know she's guilty. You know she's guilty. The law says she dies. We say she dies. What do You say?"

Jesus was quiet. Then He knelt down on the ground, the same ground from which the stones in their hands were taken. The gang was heckling now! But Jesus was still teaching. He wrote something in the dust with his finger. After writing, with their curses ringing in His ears, He stood and spoke, "He who is without sin among you, let him be the first to throw a stone at her" (John 8:7b). And once more He knelt at their feet and continued to write in the dust.

Now it became quiet. It was the Changeling's turn to squirm. What was this fool doing writing in the dust? Instead of standing and fighting, why was He kneeling before the accusers? What was He writing? The coward should be striking back! Instead He was writing in the dust, on the ground. The scribes were the ones who should have been writing. But no! The Pharisees, the old ones, they couldn't even look at what He was writing. They turned away! What was He writing?

I'll tell you what He was writing. But, first, you think about it. If you were the accuser, what would make you turn tail and run? Yes, you're right. You got it. He was writing their names and listing their sins, one by one in the dust on the temple ground.

Jesus outtricked the Trickster. He defused the Changeling's entrapment by forcing the accusers to look within. He taught us a great lesson that day. The Rabbi's response was not to throw accusations. He could have said, "Hey, which one of you was with this woman?" But He did not. He did not argue, or squirm, or curse. He did not challenge them in return. He did what rabbis do best. He simply asked a question and forced them to look for grace within. They found it and left. The challenge of change is inevitable, but spiritual progress is not. It has to do with our response to it.

When we are confronted by the Changeling's taunt, if we go into the temple rather than go out and strike back, we win. Then we will hear the thump, thump, thump of the stones falling to the floor of the temple yard. It's the home run hardball hitting the center field wall.

I know that it hurts to read this, but the importance outweighs the pain. Each morning my buddy awakens to see a stump. That's right, a stump. A stump that represents an arm and a hand that he thought were his future. The Changeling had a different idea and threw him a curve ball. Today, this morning, he looked at the stump, closed his eyes, and went within to the temple where grace lives. After the Amen, he swung his legs over the bed and went into the bathroom to brush his teeth. Oh, yes, the Changeling followed him there as well. Mark picked up the toothbrush and gripped the handle between his teeth. Then he put toothpaste on the brush. Setting down the toothpaste, he took the brush from his teeth, turned it around, and began brushing. The Changeling cursed and squirmed and fled.

Change is inevitable. Progress is not. Progress is up to us!

P.S. There is another important level to John's gospel story. Just a few feet away from where Jesus wrote in the dust on the floor of the outer courtyard with His finger was the Holy of Holies. Within that sanctuary resided the great Ark of the Covenant. Within the Ark, placed under the Mercy Seat, were the stone tablets upon which God had written the Ten Commandments. The people of Israel believed the Commandments were written by the very finger of God.

Love in the Gap
Part I

By Gary DeVaul

Love bears all things, believes all things,
hopes all things, endures all things.
- I Corinthians 13:7

During his stay in Maine Medical Center, Mark was having, and is still having, what is termed *phantom pain*. To make matters worse, he feels the pain as his mind felt it during the last moments of the crash. His brain is convinced that the wounded arm is still present and accounted for. To make matters better, Mark has learned to meditate as never before. He was taught to concentrate on the Holy Spirit as Light, just Light. He doesn't have to say anything; he just becomes quiet and concentrates on the Light.

There are many times in the Gospels that Jesus did exactly the same thing. He would go out by Himself and pray. Rarely, with the exception of the prayer in the Garden of Gethsemane and the Lord's Prayer, did He, or the gospel writers, ever tell us what He prayed for. Why were they silent on the subject? It was because Jesus was meditating on the Spirit. He was listening, not speaking. Meditation is not easy in a world filled with distractions, so Jesus went off alone. The monks of the church have been practicing meditation for years. They describe it as placing yourself between thoughts, or in "the gap" between thoughts.

Not only does Mark receive healing and comfort from his time in meditation, but I notice something wonderful about his presence afterward. His personality takes on a refreshing glow of peace and love, of a love so powerful that it lifts him to a new dimension of thought and behavior towards others. It is as if he connects with the Spirit he sees behind every face he meets. It reminds me of Jesus coming off the mount after the Transfiguration. Oh, I don't mean that Mark glows, or that he is otherworldly, but there is a visible, tangible, difference and it is wonderful.

A few years ago a university in New England purchased a powerful microscope that could actually see subatomic particles. A nuclear physicist friend shared this with me. For a nuclear scientist, subatomic particles are important things. We talked about their composition, the fact that they are alive and constantly moving, that they react to one another in harmony, and that every morsel of matter in the universe is made of them. The nuclear physicist friend who explained this phenomenon to me said, "Do you know what, Gary? It wasn't the particles themselves that I found so interesting. I had a pretty good idea what they would look like. It was the 'gaps' between the subatomic particles that took my breath away! The space between the particles was filled with a waving harmonic field of pure energy; it is that harmonic energy that held the particles together." He said that it resembled the waves of heat rising from the street on a hot day. And then he looked me square in the face and added, "I love Jesus with all my heart, and He's allowed me to see the face of God!" There were tears in his eyes. And then he said to me something so profound. "There is harmony in the gap that represents love, Gary. It's the love that's felt by the monks in the monasteries when they meditate, clear their minds, and slip into that gap between thoughts. It's the love we feel when sitting in a public place. Our minds wander or daydream, and then we see a small child, and a smile stretches our cheeks."

Divinity was a *knowing* to my friend. He is a scientist trained to believe in empirical fact, and God revealed Himself to this wonderful, faithful man in a way he could understand. He found the face of God in the gap between subatomic particles.

The love that *bears* all things is the love that Mark found in the gap. It is the love that binds us one to another. This force, or spiritual energy, is God, and it is the basis of creation. When Jesus said that My Father and I are one, He was speaking the truth. His Spirit not only connects us, it becomes us. It is our awareness of His Spirit and our relationship to Him that changes our lives.

The author of Genesis told the story of the Creation in his own way. He said God gathered the dust of the earth and formed man and then breathed the breath of life into him, and he was alive. The "breath" of life in Hebrew is the "wind" or "spirit." We are animated with the Spirit of God! And what is the tip-off to us that identifies this spiritual essence? It is that mystical connection between all living things. We become aware of it in the gap, in prayer and meditation. It is the love that *bears* all things, even the loss of arms and hands.

Some years ago in Washington, D.C., a jetliner crashed into the Potomac River. It was winter. Snow and ice filled the river. Many lost their lives in the crash. You might remember the story. It was telecast throughout the U.S. by film crews on the spot. One woman escaped the plane. She was swimming through the ice to shore. She was struggling valiantly to save her life, but hypothermia was taking its toll and she was about to drown. A rescue helicopter appeared over her, dropping a line to her with a life preserver attached. She got her arm through the life preserver and the helicopter lifted her from the water, but then her strength gave out. She plummeted back into the freezing Potomac and began to drown.

There was a man standing onshore who saw her struggle and slip beneath the ice and water. He jumped, and swam, and saved the woman. Later, as he stood wrapped in blankets at the river's edge, the reporters asked him why he did it. He said I don't know. I didn't think. I just saw her drowning – and the next thing I knew, I was with her. He didn't stop to think. The Spirit telegraphed and he jumped. That's love in the gap, the love that *bears* all things.

The love that *believes* all things is not born of naiveté. The love that *believes* all things is the love that does not judge people or circumstances. This is the love of acceptance. Lovers accept one another as they are. Love, true love, agape love, is nonjudgmental love. It does not spend its days on the telephone cursing the darkness, blaming others, or finding fault. It does not make fun of the fat lady walking down the street. For in that fat person the eye of love sees only the Spirit. The love that *believes* all things accepts people, conditions, and circumstances as they are. It does not kick the goad, curse the darkness, or make excuses for itself. It says, "Well, this is the way things are." The love that *believes* all things brings a nonjudgmental clarity to the circumstances of one's life and makes good decisions possible.

It does one more important thing. It requires that we accept responsibility for ourselves. No more blaming our parents, poverty, abuse, or the Devil. We learn to accept ourselves and our circumstances without blaming ourselves, or anyone else, and the result is peace.

Mark had asked me on several occasions to go with him to Worcester, Massachusetts, that fateful first Sunday in August 2003. It was a two and one-half hour ride each way, and I really didn't want to make the trip. Of course, now I wish that I had. Just after his accident my heart was doubly broken with guilt and anguish. One night in the hospital Mark saw it in my eyes. He took my hand and said, "Gary, there is no one to blame." Love fills the gap . . .

Love in the Gap
Part II

by Gary DeVaul

Love bears all things, believes all things,
hopes all things, endures all things.
- I Corinthians 13:7

One of many things that I observed regarding Mark's spiritual pilgrimage through the accident, his recovery, and the tremendous attention he's received since his return to California is the absence of ego. The love that *bears* all things, *believes* all things, *hopes* all things, and *endures* all things is void of ego. The hallmark of ego is fear.

There are at least two parts to our human personality. There is the spiritual self, which is the Divine representation, and there is the ego, or that which the apostle Paul referred to as "the old self" (Col. 3:9).

In short, the spiritual self is that higher self upon which Jesus meditated. It is that nonjudgmental consciousness which allows us to stand back and look at ourselves. It is that detached part of our mind that says, "You know, by all rights I shouldn't like that man. First of all, he's a politician. Second, I know he drinks too much, he's constantly exaggerating, and sometimes lies, but there is something about him that I like. I can't put my finger on it, but I like him." That's the spiritual, nonjudgmental self trying to peek through from behind the ego. That's the higher self that lives in the gap where God's harmonious love is found. It is the higher self that says, "Don't look for the bad in others in order to elevate yourself and separate yourself from them."

It is the ego that says, "I'm better." And it says it precisely because it does not believe it. The ego requires palaces, prestige, and properties, things and more things in order to elevate and separate itself to prove that it is better. It is the ego that says, "He who wins is he who has the most toys at the end of the game." For some of us, it's that regrettable voice that says, "Well, I belong to the right church, the one that really preaches the Word," as if other perceptions are of less value. The love that bears and believes all things is the love that doesn't waste time in judgment of others.

The love that *hopes* all things is a fluid, forward, expectant notion. It has its own dynamic. It is connected to all. It is void of judgment. It simply springs from between the gaps in our thoughts; it comes to us in meditation. It is the creative power of love in our present consciousness. It is the faith we have learned in the past, thrust into the future. It is that part of us that reminds us that we are all part of the field of pure possibilities. It is the love that says you are made of stardust! You can be anything! You are part and parcel of God's universe, and every element, every gift, every talent, every idea that helps, heals, or brings joy and encourages love, is yours for the asking. The love that powers hope springs from the faith of our past, and it compels one-armed organists to play organs!

This is the *hope* of the entrepreneur, the one who builds a business because he loves building, not because he loves money. This is the championship golfer who ends up winning, not because he so much wants to beat the other golfer, but because he loves playing golf. This is where we find what some would term God's will for our lives. It is the animation of God's gifts to us within the realm of our lives.

What is God's will for our lives? It is that thing you do when you lose all concept of time and you realize the day is spent and you're lost in the bliss of your endeavor. This is the love that *hopes* all things! When the runner runs, the true champion wins; he wins because he really loves to run. Oh yeah, our egos tell us that it's to separate ourselves from the other person. Our egos say that it's the manifestation of our American competitiveness, but it really is not.

Do you know the difference between millionaires who are happy and the ones who are unhappy? The difference is in motivation. If they are doing what they love to do, they are happy. If money comes, it's secondary. They are living in the loving, hopeful bliss of their spiritual selves, which are connected by their gifts directly to God's will. If they are not doing what they want to do, they are unhappy regardless of the bottom line.

When we are in the love that *bears* all things, we are aware that we are connected to everything and that the basic elements of the universe are at our disposal.

When we are in the love that *believes* all things, we are non-judgmental and free to accept life on its terms. We are not the least bit concerned with what others say about us. We have no ears for destructive criticism. We relish constructive criticism because our egos are lost and our spiritual selves have no pride of ownership. They want to incorporate that which comes from our connection to others.

When we are in the love that *hopes* all things, we cast ourselves forward into our blissful activity or vocation of love and it becomes play. We love because we love running, not just winning.

The love that *endures* is the decision to love. It is the decision to activate the love that *bears, believes,* and *hopes* all things. This is the love that says I will love regardless of the opposition, regardless of the taunts and threats.

The love that *endures* is *agape.* It is the love that is based on the decision to love. It is the love that Jesus experienced. It is the love we decide to activate in each present moment of our consciousness. It is the love that recognizes our connectedness and chooses to live in that loving moment, moment by moment. This is the decision to love. If you want to crowd out the "old self" (ego), this is how to get started.

Accept the other person as Spirit, as being part of the field of pure possibilities, part of God's universe, part of all that is, a spiritual being living in a human body. This is the love that *endures*.

This is the love that never fails, even when we find ourselves in a strange city, surrounded by doctors and nurses we don't know, lying on a gurney alone without a friend to guide and help, bleeding to death. This is the love that *bears, believes, hopes*, and *endures*, and gives permission to operate, amputating the present and casting our faith into the hands of *hope*.

Leftovers

by Gary DeVaul

Sunday night was always "Leftovers Night" when I was a kid. Mom would gather up all the leftovers in the refrigerator, warm them, mix them, stir them, and fill the house with the most incredible aromas. My mom was a great cook, and nothing could bring her talent to the forefront like leftovers.

Jesus was big on leftovers, too. The story of five loaves, two fish, and the feeding of the five thousand at Galilee is familiar to us all. In fact, it's such an important story that it's the only one of its kind repeated in all four gospels.

The disciples were tired. They had been working with Jesus all day. Teaching, preaching, healing, and comforting people and one another can make for physical and emotional exhaustion. Jesus wanted them to rest. He took them off to a quiet place beside the Sea of Galilee, only to be followed by thousands of people. Faced with all these people, the disciples came to Jesus and basically said we're beat. It's time to send these folks home to eat. They must be hungry. It's a bit like riding down U.S. Route 1 through York, Maine, with Mark. Every time we would pass Wild Willy's, his favorite hamburger place, Mark would say, "Hey, Gary, are you hungry?" The fact was that he wanted a hamburger! And in the story of the feeding of the five thousand, the disciples were saying that they were hungry and they wanted to rest. But Jesus didn't let them pass the buck onto the five thousand. He said, "You feed them."

Now the disciples knew that they didn't have two hundred denarii with which to buy bread, and they knew that Jesus knew it as well. So they threw the problem back to Jesus and said, "Shall we go buy bread?" Of course, He would have none of that and replied, "Okay, you guys, where are the leftovers?" Well, there were two measly fish and five loaves of bread, which incidentally add up to seven.

The number *seven* represents perfection to the Jews. There's an even deeper meaning here, and the numbers are the tip-off. Jesus blessed the leftovers and fed the five thousand. *Five* is symbolic of the number of books in the Torah, which is the fulfillment of the Mosaic Law that demands this kind of hospitality. When all was said and done, there were enough leftovers to fill the disciples' twelve baskets. *Twelve* represents the twelve tribes of Israel, the symbolism of which was fulfilled in the twelve disciples. The twelve baskets of leftovers were the remnants with which the disciples were to feed the world. And they are feeding the world today. This is a wonderful event that spoke directly to the hearts of the Jewish people, tapping into their knowledge of history and casting them forward in the broader context of the world. It is a story told and retold in each of the gospels, a story that incorporates a command to us today. Don't overlook the leftovers. Feed My people.

There were many nights and days that I was privileged to watch what was left of Mark rest and sleep. There was a heap of leftovers in that bed. In conversations with Jeremy McElroy, John West, and others, there was always one underlying concept. There was never any doubt, no, not one. We, like many who knew him, felt in our guts that Mark would not only survive, he would thrive! If it was said once, it was thought a hundred times. If it has to happen to someone, he's the one who can handle it. And handle it he has.

Mark has appeared on television; he's caught the attention of radio broadcasters. There are books being written about him that will inspire others to bless the leftovers and feed one another. People have been inspired to give and live differently. Concerts and benefits are being planned as I write this. Music is being composed and, most importantly, lives are being changed on the deepest levels. We are learning to lift and bless the leftovers of life because in them reside the seeds of our faith and our hope for the future of the church.

Leftovers, they're a blessing.   They are the reason for Thanksgiving!

Turning Scars into Stars

by John West

"Mark, it's good to see you," commented the Rev. Robert A. Schuller, as he warmly welcomed Mark Thallander and spoke directly to him from the pulpit of the Crystal Cathedral in Garden Grove, California. "Many people may not know the story. Mark has been an organist here for many, many years . . . . Not long ago he was in an automobile accident. He was . . . he is an organist. And he lost his arm. And I understand you're still playing the organ . . . . Your friends have composed special music for you, for a one-handed organist. Two feet, yeah. And duets. Wow. We're glad you're here, Mark. We love you."

Mark served as assistant director of music and organist at the Crystal Cathedral for eighteen years – the most defining church experience of his life to this day. And his visit there on October 5, 2003, became the most emotional reunion experience of this ordeal.

Later in the service Dr. Robert H. Schuller, on the verge of tears and remembering his own daughter's amputation experience, used Mark as a real example of turning his scars into stars. "And, again, let me repeat, Mark touches us," Dr. Schuller remarked. "I had a daughter that lost a leg and she was a runner. You lost an arm and you're an organist. We've got the faith for you, don't we? And you're showing it! You're turning your scars into stars. You'll become the world's most famous one-armed organist!"

Mark was very surprised and honored when Rev. Schuller used him as an example in his message on "Mountain Moving Faith": "And what happens when we face problems, we face pain, and we face circumstances in life which give us a left hook, and an upper cut, maybe a jab to the ribs? ... Incredible tragedies that just happen in people's lives and people get challenged and they say, Where is God? If there's such thing as mountain moving faith, where is God today? I see that through the toughest of times God is at work.

"Sitting in the front row is Mark Thallander. Mark is one of the greatest organists you could hear. He made this organ sing like you can't believe. And not once but regularly. He'd practice on this thing for hours. Not once in awhile but daily. Not long ago he was in an automobile accident. And during the accident his arm got twisted and mangled by the seat belt. And the doctors couldn't save his arm. And he lost his arm. And we say, Where is God? Where is the justice? How could God do this to this man? The positive thoughts produce positive reactions. Possibility thinkers find the possibilities in the most unlikely circumstances. And now today, if I believe this is still true, Mark is planning on a tour, an organ tour, am I right? And you're going to be traveling around the nation doing concerts. And people are writing special music, and God has turned this negative into an incredible positive. It's hard to fathom the magnitude and the power of God."

Following the service a gala luncheon was to be celebrated over at the local watering hole, Hof's Hut, with around thirty people in attendance. Prior to Mark going there he was assailed by many well-wishers at the church who told him how meaningful the articles written by Gary DeVaul have been to them. But the crowning touch was having an unexpected and private prayer moment with Dr. Schuller. It is a moment and a time Mark will not soon forget.

From the Pew @ Lake Avenue

by Alicia Steinhaus

For years, I sat in the pew at Lake Avenue Church (LAC) in Pasadena, California, and marveled at the glorious sounds coming from our organ. Truth be told, it was the organ, and the music, that was the biggest drawing card when I started going to Lake. It's a wonderful Casavant instrument with 127 ranks of pipes and sounds that only begin to display the vast depth of our God; from sweet, tender-loving whispers to great blasts of righteous anger. God so wonderfully reveals Himself to me in the organ; yet I know it is but a glimpse. Sunday after Sunday Mark Thallander, our director of music and organist, would lead us in praise and reflection, encompassing every imaginable emotion in between.

What he did for us on the organ during services was only the tip of the iceberg of all that he did for us at Lake. For many he was the encourager who kept us going through the discouraging times. He encouraged the young musicians to persevere. Truly a world-class musician, he was never proud or arrogant, but down-to-earth, kind, and loving. As wonderfully gifted as he is, he never once let anyone feel that their gift was any less than his. When he sensed God was calling him elsewhere several years back, I was sad. I knew he would not be gone from my life, just gone from my weekly worship experience.

This fall [2003], Dr. Gordon Kirk, LAC senior pastor, has been leading us through a series entitled "Loving Community." For seven weeks we have been exploring the commandment that we "love one another" as Jesus has loved us. Last weekend was the first part of exploring comfort, God's compassion and comfort of us, and ours of each other. This weekend, the second part, we saw firsthand through a life experience, Mark's story, an example of our study in comfort and compassion. LAC welcomed Mark back with open arms – arms that greeted him with stirring standing ovations as we praised God that Mark once again stood in our midst. We audibly showed how much we loved Mark! Saturday night and two Sunday morning services, each of them unique, each of them individually blessed with an overwhelming evidence of God's love and comfort and its earthly embodiment in those around us, as Pastor Kirk led us through Mark's story.

There was moving video of Mark playing and directing – everything from the Crystal Cathedral, to our own services at Lake, to a fantastic Christmas production at the Church on the Way in Van Nuys, California. It did a great job of introducing Mark to those unfamiliar with him and his ministry. There was a clip from the service at the Crystal Cathedral when Dr. Robert H. Schuller greeted Mark from the pulpit – a very poignant moment as Dr. Schuller reflected on his daughter Carol's loss of her leg as a runner and now Mark's loss of an arm as an organist. Dr. Schuller was choked up. Yet he stated with confidence that our faith was bigger and that Mark's scars were being turned into stars already; he has become the world's most famous one-armed organist! There were pictures of the Toyota 4Runner, the ten monkey butlers from LAC organist Julian Revie, and friends who stood close by Mark literally in those difficult days following the accident.

But most of all, there was the testimony of a man who has faced some of the darkest moment's life could ever hold with strength and grace that evidence a divine comfort administered through earthly angels of compassion. When the chips were down, the promises flooded back.

> *Day by day and with each passing moment,*
> *Strength I find to meet my trials here;*
> *Trusting in my Father's wise bestowment,*
> *I've no cause for worry or for fear.*[1]

When Mark could hardly stand on his own without toppling over, it was:

> *Jesus is all the world to me,*
> *My life, my joy, my all;*
> *He is my strength from day to day,*
> *Without Him I would fall.[2]*

Standing alone, unsure of his balance, at the top of a scary flight of stairs, as only Mark could say, "Okay, Jesus, here we go!" Mark showed us all how those familiar, comforting words became so VERY real.

He eased listeners into talk of his "new arm" with its multiple hands, explaining that one would be his utility, hold-the-bucket hand and another would be his "party hand" with a sensor in the thumb to alert the four fingers if a glass being held needed to be grasped harder when it was being filled. He even told of his "keyboard hand" and how it will allow him to play a fifth! As you might expect, Mark's humor was intact throughout as he stated he would carry them in a "handbag" and would now truly be able to offer anyone "a hand"!

Always in the forefront was the reality that Jesus IS strength in weakness. Even when our hearts are breaking, He is our comfort.

> *Hallelujah! What a Savior!*
> *Hallelujah! What a friend!*
> *Saving, helping, keeping, loving;*
> *He is with me to the end![3]*

We sang in the opening hymn, "A mighty fortress is our God, a bulwark never failing." The choir finished off the message of hope with "He's Never Failed Me Yet," one of the most powerful music moments so far this year. Lastly, in a particularly moving moment, we all listened in wonderment to the Widor Toccata as Julian Revie shared the majesty of God through the Casavant organ.

As I stood at the CD table in the lobby, people commented on how moving the service was. What they had expected to be a very hard, very sad time was one full of hope, promise, and great joy! One person even left a note saying they had seen God's glory in Mark's eyes that morning. He was in his truest form, full of grace, well-rounded with his famous wit. He totally engaged each service as he shared how God was with him through each step and has only just started; the best is definitely yet to come!

And of course there was an extremely fun meal on Saturday evening after the service, with Pastor Kirk and his wife, Patricia, their son, Jonathan, Pastor Jerry Johnson, and friends Julian Revie, Janelle Grose, Neal Noorlag, and my husband, Jeff, and myself. It was NOT the usual hamburger and chocolate ice cream – it was an absolutely fabulous meal at Panda Inn, full of every type of meat and vegetable you can imagine. The finish? Not chocolate, but Green Tea ice cream – unless you ordered the vanilla with chocolate syrup, which of course was Mark's choice.

But the obvious theme throughout all the events of the weekend – God is not through with Mark Thallander yet! If you thought what God did with Mark before was amazing and unbelievable, well, you'd better hang on tight because the best is really yet to come, and it promises to be the ultimate "E ticket."

1. "Day By Day and With Each Passing Moment" by Lina Sandell, tr. A.L. Skoog.
2. "Jesus Is All the World to Me" by Will L. Thompson.
3. "Jesus! What a Friend for Sinners" by J. Wilbur Chapman.

Hope in Time of Adversity

by Mark Thallander

On a beautiful autumn Sunday afternoon, November 23, 2003, the Thornton School of Music of the University of Southern California (USC) offered a concert titled "Hope in Time of Adversity." It was skillfully presented by the 100-member University Chorus and Orchestra, conducted by Granville Oldham, Jr., in the historic sanctuary of the United University Church, located on the USC campus near downtown Los Angeles.

Having observed Granville's dynamic choral conducting technique one summer at a Presbyterian Association of Musicians music and worship conference in Albuquerque, New Mexico, where we were on staff together, I had been looking forward to serving as his accompanist for the University Chorus for the 2003-04 academic year. Even though I was unable to fulfill those duties because of my accident, I was indeed honored and humbled to be a special guest at the fall concert and was certainly touched by the music and inspired by the texts to move forward with my own musical career. I am indebted to Granville for his thoughtfulness in dedicating "Hope in Time of Adversity" to me and for his kind remarks at the program.

The first concert selection was a cantata, *Nun ist das Heil und die Kraft* (BWV 50), by Johann Sebastian Bach (1685-1750). The text is based on Revelation 12:10 and is translated from the German: "Now is come hope/salvation and strength, and the kingdom and the power of our God and of his Christ." It brought back to my mind the summer when I had taken a graduate course at USC called The Cantatas of J. S. Bach. How I love Bach's music!

Missa in Angustiis (Hob. XXII:11) by Franz Joseph Haydn (1732-1809) followed the Bach cantata. This "Mass in Adversity" (or "Mass in Time of Fear") contains one of my favorite musical settings of the *Kyrie*. The only Greek words in the Latin Mass, *Kyrie eleison, Christe eleison* ("Lord, have mercy, Christ, have mercy"), became a very personal prayer for me as I waited for the paramedics to extricate me from the Toyota 4Runner just a few months prior in Maine.

"Hold On!" by Moses George Hogan (1957-2003) was the final exclamation point of the program. The words gripped my heart: "...keep on climbin' an' don't you tire, 'cause ev'ry rung goes higher an' higher! Keep yo' hand on de plow, an' you hold on!" Because Moses Hogan was such a well-known and amazing arranger of spirituals, singers throughout the country had been praying for his healing, but the Lord took Moses home earlier that year. In my mind I pictured Moses smiling from the heavenly realm as the University Chorus communicated his setting with such passion.

The following is the very kind and gracious tribute reprinted from the concert program that afternoon:

Mark Alan Thallander
Dedicatee

Mark Alan Thallander is a talented organist and educator. He received his bachelor of arts in humanities from Vanguard University, his master's degree in music from California State University, and was accepted (Fall 2003) into the doctor of musical arts program in sacred music at the USC Thornton School of Music.

Mr. Thallander was the assistant director of music and organist at The Crystal Cathedral for eighteen years. He has held positions at Menlo Park Presbyterian Church, Vanguard University,

Glendale Presbyterian Church, and Glendale Community College. He also served three years as Dean of the Orange County Chapter of the American Guild of Organists. He is a member of the board of directors for Vanguard University Alumni Association, the organ editor for Fred Bock Music Company, and organ music reviewer for *Creator* magazine.

Mark Alan Thallander has published four books of hymn arrangements for congregational singing and two recordings of hymn improvisations. In addition to publishing, he has lectured on the use of organ in blended worship for the National Convention of the Royal Canadian College of Organists in Ottawa, Ontario.

Thallander performed on the live recording of The Crystal Cathedral's 20th Anniversary Concert of the Hazel Wright Organ and at The Cathedral of Our Lady of the Angels, Los Angeles. He has also performed at St. Patrick's Cathedral, New York City, and at Carnegie Hall.

Mark Thallander was to accompany the University Chorus this year but had an accident that prohibited him from fulfilling that commitment. The chorus missed a great opportunity to work with a talented musician with skill, integrity, a sense of humor, and a resilient spirit.

Man's Triumph Strikes a Chord

by Steve Scauzillo

[Steve Scauzillo is the editorial page editor for the San Gabriel Valley Newspaper Group (Pasadena Star News, San Gabriel Valley Tribune, Whittier Daily News). This column was originally published Saturday, Dec. 6, 2003, by the SGVN Newspaper Group and was reprinted with permission on the Lake Avenue Church Web site. It is reprinted here with permission.]

In the midst of performing a duet of "Christmas Fantasy," Mark Thallander's right hand traveled across the keyboard of the massive, 7,072-pipe Casavant organ at Lake Avenue Church and headed for the wrong note.

The organist had played the piece a thousand times, but this time was different. It was the first time he had played the tune since losing his left arm in an automobile accident. The music for the concert was rewritten for two organists, or (as Thallander puts it) for three hands and four feet.

"It wasn't the melody line. It was the line I used to play. It was a scary moment but overall, it had a very exciting effect," he said, minutes after the afternoon audience gave him a standing ovation.

Thallander is indeed heading in a new direction, one with considerable bumps in the road. The 53-year-old organist is navigating his new road map using his strong Christian faith and the support of family and friends.

Some in the audience called him inspirational. I asked him if what he is doing is courageous.

"I would say that this is part of my journey," he said. "Now, I can just go along for the ride, wherever God takes me."

Before Aug. 3, the day of his car crash, Thallander was a renowned organist who played 18 years at the Crystal Cathedral in Garden Grove, as a guest artist at St. Patrick's Cathedral in New

York City and many other landmark churches, and locally, in Pasadena's Lake Avenue Church from 1995 to 1999.

Then, while on a concert tour in New England, Thallander's Toyota 4Runner hydroplaned off the interstate during a fierce summer rainstorm and skidded on its side through a guardrail. His arm was crushed and he lost 70 percent of his blood.

When he arrived at the hospital in Portland, Maine, he told the surgeons he was an organist, and begged them to save his arm. But saving his life meant amputating his left arm.

How could a loving God allow an organist – His organist – to lose his gift of music? I asked him that because frankly, it was a question running through my mind as I sat and listened to him struggle through the organ duet.

"I remember Robert [H.] Schuller would say, 'Look at what you have left, don't look at what you've lost.' I had no internal injuries. I had no cuts. I lost 70 percent of my blood. It's amazing what I have left. God has a reason for me to be alive," Thallander answered.

I went to Lake Avenue Church to listen to Christmas music, hoping for a touch of Christmas spirit. I came back to the newsroom with a lot more than a warm feeling.

Don Pascoe, a musician and West Covina resident, said he was "sick to his stomach for three days" when he first learned Thallander had lost his arm. But he came away from the concert Thursday with a different feeling. "The message is determination, one of personal healing and miraculous recovery," he said.

Thallander himself said audience members in Pasadena and at the Crystal Cathedral where he played, told him his example made them more confident they could navigate their own troubles. "My prayer is that whatever their passion is, they can move through their obstacles and fulfill that dream."

With the help of his friend and colleague, LAC's church organist [Julian Revie], he played more confidently through the Christmas carol medley, crossing his body with his right hand to pull out the stops before launching into the familiar melody of "Hark! The Herald Angels Sing."

Julian Revie and Mark perform a duet at an Advent Recital at Lake Avenue Church in Pasadena, California.

Thallander was alone on the day of his accident, pinned between the car and the roadway, and he was bleeding to death. Then he heard someone instructing him to turn off the car's ignition to prevent a car fire. The voice continued speaking to him, comforting him, telling him, "The paramedics are almost here – I can see their lights." Only neither the police nor the fire department nor the Maine Highway Patrol have a record of anyone calling 911. And there were no witnesses to the single-car crash.

The music from the colossal pipe organ talked about angels and a message of hope. It's a message Thallander knows firsthand.

"At Christmastime, I think about angels. I believe God sent an angel to take care of me. Yes, angels are available," he said.

Thallander's friends are rewriting music for one hand for his future concerts. He has an invitation to play Duruflé's "Requiem" at Carnegie Hall in March and, appropriately, at the Cathedral of Our Lady of the Angels in Los Angeles.

Life's Not Fair

by Mark Thallander

Donna Grimm, who served with distinction for nearly twenty years in the pastoral care ministry of the Crystal Cathedral, warmly greeted me as I answered the phone. She had called to tell me that the committee had unanimously voted to present the annual "Life's Not Fair but God is Good" award to me. We rejoiced together over the phone. After we ended our conversation, I sat down and was so overcome by the love of my friends at the Crystal Cathedral to do such a meaningful thing for me. I was overwhelmed, humbled, and honored.

Family and friends also considered this a very special occasion. My cousin Diane planned a special road trip for her mom, my mom, and my cousin Karen's mom. From Northern California they came and stayed with Karen and her husband, Dean, in San Juan Capistrano. I can only imagine the fun those three sisters had traveling with Diane! It was quite a weekend. It was wonderful to have my mother, Aunt Eva, Aunt Dodie, plus many relatives and friends there in Garden Grove, California, to see me receive the award and to hear me play an organ solo. All of these people had surrounded me with prayer, and it was a joy to be able to celebrate together on the beautiful Crystal Cathedral campus ignited with an atmosphere of possibility thinking.

The three Branvold sisters: Delores Smith, Mae Thallander, and Evelyn Sommer

The award, which has a prominent place on my piano, has engraved on it 2 Corinthians 4:8-9, a Scripture passage which has become very meaningful to me in my daily Christian walk.

"Life's Not Fair but God is Good"
Awarded to
Mark Thallander

"afflicted…but not crushed; perplexed, but not driven to despair; struck down, but not destroyed."
2 Corinthians 4:8-9

International Conference on Care and Kindness
Crystal Cathedral
March 12, 2004

Passion

by Gary DeVaul

Passion is the kindling force behind an idea, person, place, or thing. Lovers find passion in the sexual synergism of a relationship. Painters are fired with passion at the sight of a face or the drama inherent in a sunrise. The architect's passion gives birth to a form-like feeling that begs first for paper and then bursts into brick and mortar, or titanium, and we have the Guggenheim Bilbao or the Walt Disney Concert Hall in Los Angeles. Musicians find their passion is torched in the organization of fragmented sound into a meaningful whole, a whole that is mathematically succinct and yet moves the listener to a place of transcendence where logic is no longer necessary. Those of you who have heard my friend Mark Thallander play for a church service or a concert know that his passion for the worship of God comes through when he plays the organ.

Passion comes in all shapes and sizes. It comes to all kinds of people, for a hundred reasons and a thousand different manifestations that reflect the truth of an individual. Passion is the kindling of a life on the cross because the only prerequisite to passion is sacrifice. And the only true sacrifice is the sacrifice of self.

Of course, passion is the "name of the game" today. There's lots of money being made on the Passion of Christ these days. That's not necessarily bad, but nevertheless it might behoove us to remember that passion always has to do with someone, or something else, beside ourselves. A passion for "self" is self-absorption, the manifestation of an unhealthy ego. I'm glad to be writing today. I'm glad to get out of myself for a while and think of your hopes and dreams. You see, I have been a bit under the weather lately, and when you're ill, it's difficult to think of anything or anyone, save yourself and your own pain. And that never makes me very comfortable. After all, I know what a jerk I really am, and spending time fussing about me is about as helpful as spitting into the wind. Our passion must be for someone, or something else, besides ourselves.

Jesus' Passion had nothing to do with Himself as a person; it had everything to do with us, His brothers and sisters. Jesus was no friend of death and dying. He was its enemy. Jesus was, and is, the remedy for death. Nothing illustrates this better than His reaction to the death of his friend Lazarus. When Jesus heard of Lazarus' illness and came to Bethany to visit, He found that his friend had died. He passed through the mourners, those bringing food to the family. He passed through the relatives and friends who gathered to mourn, and one has the definite feeling that Jesus was not happy as He approached the grave with Martha.

Most of you know that the shortest verse in the Bible is John 11:35, "Jesus wept." But what you may not know is that the Aramaic word used for "wept" was a strange choice in that it was the word used to describe an angry warhorse snorting, tears running down its face, rearing up for battle. This is not the portrait of some weepy creature. This is a portrait of an angry, livid man about to do battle. The shortest verse in the Bible gives us huge insights into the personality of Jesus. He was capable of anger and rage. He was also capable of great love. For it was His love of life and His love for His friend Lazarus that Jesus does battle with death. For it was with a great shout that Jesus called Lazarus from the tomb. There was no mistaking what Jesus wanted. He wanted Lazarus back, and the voice that had called the earth into being shook the foundations of the tomb. You can almost see the sand and dust falling from the ceiling as the grave trembled at the sound of the Creation voice. And Lazarus arose! He came out into the sunlight, they set him free of his grave cloths, and he was alive!

This, too, was Jesus' Passion, for it was a premonition of what would shortly take place in His own life. His Passion would soon be ours, and we, too, would be free of death. But as for now, it was all about Lazarus, all about the other guy.

That's where passion begins. It starts with an idea that relates to people. It's primarily about the other person, not about us. The problem is that if we are distracted by ourselves, we cannot hear Him call. Remember when you were a kid in school and you were talking to a friend in class when you were supposed to be listening to the teacher? Remember when the teacher called on you and you not only didn't know the answer to the question, but you didn't even hear your name called? Remember how your face would get hot and red and you would shrivel up in embarrassment?

I cannot speak for you. I can only speak for myself. When He calls, "Gary," I want to hear Him call. And that won't happen if I'm listening to myself or shooting my mouth off, will it?

Note to the Reader: Gary wrote the above article in March 2004, less than three months after he had been diagnosed with multiple myeloma.

From Requiem to Resurrection

by Jacque I. Blauvelt

Vision. (vizh'n) something seen in a dream or trance, an image or series of images seen in a dream or trance, often interpreted as having religious, revelatory, or prophetic significance.

I have never considered myself visionary, revelatory, or prophetic. Religious? Yes, if the word points to the belief in the virgin birth, life, death, and resurrection of Christ Jesus. It has been my distinct privilege to be involved in an Assemblies of God church, especially within the area of music. As a registered nurse and a licensed minister, music has been my retreat, a solace and joy of worship. It has been said that music is the language of the soul. Nothing could be closer to the truth. It comes from the soul and speaks to it all at once. No one escapes the reach of music, whether producing or simply listening to it. Perhaps the medical side of me and the music ministry part of me drew me into Mark Thallander's plight from the moment I heard of his accident.

I was in the audience the night Mark played for the reunited Revivaltime Choir during the Assemblies of God General Council week in Washington, D.C. The day we left Washington, August 3, 2003, was a dreary, overcast day with the threat of stormy weather on the airport horizon. We were anxious to be in the air and away from the storms. Little did I realize the extent of concern those very storms were about to produce. Little did I know how much Mark would be in our prayers for the many weeks that followed.

It was months later that Mark was with us at Central Assembly of God in Springfield, Missouri. He had and continues to be a welcome friend and guest during Easter. It just would not seem like an Easter service without Mark at the organ. Normally I'm carried away, along with the rest of the choir altos, with the reverberating sound from the organ speakers right behind us. But on this particular Sunday, we had been dismissed early enough for me to run around to the organ side of the balcony so I could get a bird's eye view of Mark at the organ console. This was his first Easter with only one arm. I could only imagine what might be going through his mind. After all he had been through, I knew from a medical standpoint that it was still too early to be emotionally adjusted to such a physical change, not to mention a change that so greatly affected his life work and passion. From the very first note, I was in tears.

As I watched, listened, and cried from my isolated spot above and slightly behind Mark, I saw a mist begin to form behind him. I was transfixed as it slowly grew to a small cloud of vapor. Then from within the cloud a left arm extended out to Mark's back and hovered over his left shoulder. The arm was draped in cloth, and the entire arm and hand, cloth included, were as transparent as the mist. The only color was on Mark's left shoulder. The hand emitted a shadow of bright light directly on Mark's left shoulder as if resting there. As Mark played, the hand remained. As Mark ended the last triumphant chord, the hand retreated to the misty cloud and slowly vanished altogether.

It was then that I realized what I had seen. In all honesty, I was reluctant to look around, concerned that my face would give me away. Again, I am not prone to visions of any kind, and to be sure, no one would believe me if I were to speak up. As the morning service ended, I mustered my courage grounded in the confidence of what my eyes had truly seen (knowing my limited imagination could have never concocted such a thing!) and shared what I saw with a dear friend sitting nearby. Still shaken by it, I could hardly speak. The tears would not stop. She encouraged me to tell Mark.

I waited until the last person had spoken with him. Mark had been surrounded at the close of the service. I caught him just as he was gathering his music to leave. How does a person tell another person a visionary story and somehow convey how *true* it is? I'm sure my voice trembled as I tried to explain what I saw while he played. Soon the tears flowed freely down both of our faces. Mark told me how he had sought God to somehow "fix the music" so that no one would miss what his left hand would have played, how he had asked God to "*be* his left hand." Now the revelation was clear. God had done exactly that.

To this day, I haven't seen another misty cloud or hand form before my eyes. But as with all things touched by God, the effects of the touch of that hand are everywhere. As Mark continues to play out his love for Christ on the organ keys, God's hand still rests on that left shoulder. I can hear it every time Mark plays.

Affirming Faith and Life

by Eric Dale Knapp

As I stood in the intersection of 36th and Broadway in New York City, I heard Jeremy McElroy on my cell phone tell me that Mark had been in an accident. Then the question, What happened?

As Jeremy began to share the events of August 3, 2003, I was stopped cold in my tracks, standing in the middle of Broadway, frozen, unable to comprehend Mark's situation. My good friend Terre Johnson was with me, and he was screaming at me to get out of the street. However, there I was, paralyzed by the statement, "They had to amputate his left arm, but Mark will survive." As Terre pulled me out of the intersection, I simply stood and looked at my friend, unable to speak.

How could this great tragedy have occurred? How could God allow this to happen to a faithful servant? Why? Mark had just played the organ at Carnegie Hall on June 8, 2003, in a performance of Beethoven's *Mass in C,* which I had the privilege to conduct.

Once I came to my senses, it was clear that Mark's extended community of friends and loved ones would need to help. To this day the number of people from across the country who prayed and became the community that would be there to support Mark in this time humbles me.

As we walked into the week following the accident, I began to make telephone calls to choir directors in Southern California regarding the opportunity to present a benefit concert on Mark's behalf. By a divine plan I was scheduled to conduct the Duruflé *Requiem* at Carnegie Hall on April 16, 2004, and the choirs associated with this festival were primarily from Southern California. With all of this in mind, I flew to Maine to visit Mark and spend time with Gary DeVaul discussing the possibilities.

Gary DeVaul was a force of nature filled with life and zest.

Everyone agreed that the benefit concert concept was a good next step. Gary discussed the idea with Frederick Swann, the Crystal Cathedral's organist emeritus, and we all agreed to proceed with the development of the Affirmation of Faith and Life benefit concert. Interestingly enough, I thought that by suggesting we perform the Duruflé *Requiem*, the choirs planning to sing the piece in New York would be prepared and directors would not need to teach additional music. However, Fred rose up in righteous indignation and said to Gary, "The *Requiem* . . . he's not dead . . . why on God's green earth would we sing a REQUIEM!" Hence, Affirmation of Faith and Life was developed, and an eclectic program of varied repertoire celebrating God's grace emerged.

Gary minced no words about what the program should be. We needed to celebrate and rejoice that Mark is with us. So off I went into months of Gary badgering every single livid idea and program piece suggested. I thought it would never end! However, through it all Gary was extremely compassionate and thoughtful regarding how we should proceed.

We selected Proverbs 3:5-6 (NIV) as our focal point:

> *Trust in the Lord with all your heart,*
> *and lean not on your own understanding;*
> *In all your ways acknowledge him,*
> *and he will make your paths straight.*

Theology and music began to merge with this Scripture in place, and our conversations traveled through devotions, hymnody, choral music, and poetry as we began to develop the program for Affirmation of Faith and Life.

Gary was my partner in ministry throughout the processes of developing the benefit concert. Gary reviewed all of the hymn choices and began to write the initial script that would weave the benefit concert together. Gary and I prayed, laughed, and cried through the entire process. Gary's excitement and commitment carried us forward during the many labor-intensive months of planning and organization.

Personally, I needed to be able to help Mark, and the benefit concert was something that could be possible, given Mark's association with so many wonderful musicians in Southern California. So one telephone call at a time, I proceeded to contact each director with the news of Mark's accident and to invite them to join me in presenting a benefit concert in March of 2004 at Lake Avenue Church in Pasadena, California. The response was unanimous, and so began the work to organize this event with the goal of creating financial support for Mark. Every single person contacted responded in the affirmative. Over 800 singers turned out to participate in this event. The concert of worship was exhilarating and provided such an important moment for the community to gather, pray, and celebrate God's ever-bearing power to sustain us.

As each choir was confirmed and each person invited accepted the call, Gary and I rejoiced daily over the telephone. I in New York City and Gary by the sea in Ogunquit, Maine. It was as if we were in the same room. The connection was through the Holy Spirit. Gary continued to lift up the fact that God was on our side and had given us the wisdom, gifts, and intelligence with which to create this amazing ministry of faith in daily life. Even when Gary became ill with multiple myeloma, he was the greatest cheerleader of this project. He would scream at me over the telephone in excitement, and of course all while I reminded him that I was a conductor with the ability to hear him if he could just reign in his enthusiasm a bit. His capacity to interface with the Southern California communities brought great insight and inspired and nurtured everyone touched by accepting the call to service!

The benefit concert evening was uplifting and healing for so many. Mark was back on his feet and played the organ brilliantly. Gary was on the podium in rare form, tantalizing the audience with his wit and leading us to better understand a God of great might and courage. As the program unfolded, it was as if the angels were present. When the congregation joined in the singing of the hymns, it felt as though we were singing with the heavenly consort. Voices, organ, brass, and percussion all united in one voice of worship. It was glorious. Indeed, in music we found God and God found us!

The angels gathered around Mark, and angels on earth gathered to sing the Affirmation of Faith and Life. God's presence with us through the holy angels is significant. Surely there are many ways in which we sense that *angels* are present with us.

We often compare the sounds of the voices and instruments in worship to the *music of the angels.* As the community gathered, we celebrated the life and music making of Mark Thallander, one who has brought angelic sounds to our ears for many years in Southern California and beyond.

We often credit the presence of *guardian angels* when death is averted and life is extended. Angelic intervention spared Mark's life after a terrifying accident and will continue to help him rebuild all that was shattered on that roadside in Maine.

And we often think that we are *walking among angels* when we see the best of human nature rise to the occasion of helping a brother in a time of need. This was such a time, and we were called to an angelic challenge of helping to reestablish the well-being of one who has contributed so much to ours.

The question was: *Listen. Angels are singing. Will you join the song?*

The angels sang! God's people responded! Angels of Christian compassion were summoned and a community emerged. From tragedy to triumph the words *Soli Deo Gloria* have been echoed across the country with the development and success of the Mark Thallander Foundation. Yet another gift from God, I am convinced!

It was the song that united all of us in ministry and continues to tether us in the Scriptures. We are never alone. The psalmist

affirms that God is ever with us and will sustain us always! I find
the text of Paul Christiansen's "My Song in the Night" to be a
poignant prayer reminding us of our compass of faith and security
in God's love.

> *O Jesus, my Savior, my song in the night,*
> *come to us with Thy tender love, my soul's delight.*
> *Unto Thee, O Lord, in affliction I call,*
> *my comfort by day and my song in the night.*
> *O why should I wander, an alien from Thee,*
> *or cry in the desert Thy face to see?*
> *My comfort and joy, my soul's delight,*
> *O Jesus, my Savior, my song in the night.*

Amen.

Julian Revie, organist from Lake Avenue
Church in Pasadena, California, and
Mark's duet partner

Mark joins John West at the keyboard.

Lois Bock, Julie Alley, Randy Alley (Mark's prosthetist), and David Leestma enjoy time together during a gathering the night before the Affirmation of Faith and Life benefit concert.

Humbled and in Awe

by Jeremy McElroy

Imagine arriving in Pasadena to attend the Affirmation of Faith and Life benefit concert on the perfect evening: mild temperatures (it's Southern California, of course!), clear skies, and eager anticipation of what is to come. You know that it will be crowded, and you are prepared to park several blocks away and take the free shuttle bus to Lake Avenue Church. Surely there will be a lot of people. You step off the bus, and your field of vision is assaulted by a sea of black and white. What is that massive creature? you ask. Why, it's the Festival Choir! Over 800 singers, representing nineteen churches, colleges, and communities from California, Canada, New York, and my personal favorite, Pittsburgh, Pennsylvania. How will they all fit on the stage? you wonder.

After your obligatory blinks of awe and wow, you proceed inside to the lobby. It is here that you observe, and perhaps discover for the first time, the many areas of ministry that Mark Thallander uses to share his love of our Lord. His newest book of hymn arrangements, *Organ Hymns of Faith, Volume 3,* is nicely displayed with two other editions of like material. Several CDs of solo organ, solo piano, collaborative keyboard concerts, and choral ensembles are being offered. An exciting new entrant is the very recently published book *Champions* by the Reverend Gary DeVaul. A collection of meditative and devotional writings surrounding Mark's accident and ensuing journey, this book is hot off the press.

Proceeding into the sanctuary, you are again struck by wonderment. There are over 3,000 other attendees who have come to show their support for Mark. All these people have come to participate in probably the largest group affirmation of musical encouragement Mark has ever experienced. Can you imagine entering a room filled with over 4,000 singers and guests gathered to show how much they love you? I dare say Mark has probably never been touched quite like he was on Sunday evening, March 21, 2004.

Some highlights of the evening were two Max Reger organ solos performed by Mark's long-time friend Frederick Swann. Readings from the gospel and participatory prayers of St. Francis of Assisi and the Lord's Prayer with the congregation afforded everyone the opportunity to contribute to the service. Some spectacular choral works were the thrust of the evening including the magnificent "Sanctus" from *Requiem*, op. 9 by Maurice Duruflé, and "Antiphon" from *Five Mystical Songs* by Ralph Vaughan Williams, as well as arrangements of two very comforting hymn texts, "My Song in the Night" and "My Shepherd Will Supply My Need." We were honored to have the very gifted Jubilant Sykes sing "A City Called Heaven." Some powerful moments occurred with the congregational singing of hymns arranged into works for choir, organ, and brass, including John Rutter's "All Creatures of Our God and King" and "O God, Our Help in Ages Past," plus Dan Bird's arrangement of "Great Is Thy Faithfulness," conducted by Dan himself.

Maestro Eric Dale Knapp, another long-time friend of Mark's and the man behind the concept for the evening, conducted nearly all of the choral works. John West, Julian Revie, and Christian Elliott accompanied on the organ, and Peter Green accompanied on the piano. Linda White, Rebecca Sloat, and Amy Barnhart offered their talents on flute, oboe, and voice, respectively. The Westminster Brass was spectacular in its ensemble playing. Hanan Yaqub led the Chancel Choir of Trinity United Presbyterian Church, and Jeremy Langill conducted the Master's Ringers of Lake Avenue Church. The whole evening was led by two wonderful people: the Reverend Gary DeVaul and Ms. Stephanie Edwards, whose motivational and inspired words seamlessly connected each event and compelled us to worship.

Without question, though, the pinnacle of the evening was a performance of Mark Thallander's Toccata on "Hymn to Joy," arranged for two feet, one human right hand, and one prosthetic left hand. Mark was the arranger. And Mark was the performer. And we were mesmerized. Not once did the piece sound lacking in any way. It was full, powerful, assertive, and glorious. Mark reworked the piece shortly after returning to California last fall, and it was quite spectacular with just one hand and two feet. However, since he recently debuted the newest addition to his home and body (the prosthetic arm, of course), it was only fitting that he teach it to play the organ! So Mark made some changes to the end of the piece and utilized his keyboard hand. (He actually will have three different hands for different functions.) The fingers are in the position of a fifth on the keyboard, and when he leaned his shoulder, the sound grew and every soul was moved. God can use *anything* to His glory, even plastic hands. The piece ended, and the voices of 4,000 changed people erupted in a roar of applause and emotional outpouring.

Mark could not have been more humbled and touched, and I could not have been more in awe.

The Festival Choir at the Affirmation of Faith and Life benefit at Lake Avenue Church in Pasadena, California

Maestro Eric Dale Knapp during the Affirmation of Faith and Life concert

Gary DeVaul joins Eric Dale Knapp on stage during the benefit concert.

John West is welcomed to the microphone.

Gary DeVaul autographs copies of his book, Champions, *which "debuted" at the Affirmation of Faith and Life benefit.*

Mark takes a bow after the presentation of his signature piece, Toccata on "Hymn to Joy."

Champions Gary DeVaul and Mark Thallander celebrate the "victory" after Mark's performance.

With Praise for Our Composer

by Greg Asimakoupoulos

Sometimes our lives appear destined to be played in a minor key.
When major traumas cause us to pull out all the stops
and still our best efforts are not enough,
we grieve (and for good reason).

God can seem silent.
But, listen.
The one whose steady hand
takes delight in scoring the melody line of our lives
is holding us with everlasting arms
that will never let us go.

Mark, His Words . . .

"Nothing can separate us
from the love of God
that is in Christ Jesus our Lord . . . "

Even when all that is left is our right hand,
the Master Composer envelopes us
with His calming (yet confident) presence
as He proceeds to make sense of the bass clef
and incorporate a counterpoint melody
alongside our best offering.

Mark, His Words . . .

"My grace is sufficient for you,
for my power is made perfect in weakness . . . "
In our silence, His beauty is heard.
Through accidentals and unexpected passages,
the beauty of the entire composition is clarified.

Man with a Musical Mission

by Rosemary Jackson

B efore Mark Thallander was born, his mother and her church pianist, Mavis Thompson, in Grand Forks, North Dakota, prayed daily that this "baby" would be a pianist for the glory of God. Those prayers were answered! When Mark is asked, "When did you decide to go into musical ministry?" his response always is, "It was decided for me. It was a calling from God."

The year Mark was born, *Revivaltime* began broadcasting its weekly radio program across the nation (and around the world), and Mark grew up listening to that musical sound.

The night before his graduation from Lincoln High School in Stockton, California, the Revivaltime Choir was singing at Bethel Temple in nearby Hayward, and Mark persuaded his parents to take him. It was both an exciting drive and an exciting service for young Mark. He listened intently to the choir and watched the pianist. Grace Blunt, a friend from Lincoln Neighborhood Church in Stockton, accompanied them. She took Mark immediately to the director, Cyril McLellan, and said, "Mark will be playing the piano for you this fall." Mark would never have marched up to Cyril McLellan to introduce himself. It took the courage and tenacity of Grace Blunt! Taken somewhat by surprise, Director McLellan replied, "My pianist is leaving at the end of the summer tour. Audition for me after the service." This seventeen-year-old became a man with a mission!

Mark made plans. He applied to attend Central Bible College (CBC). The day before he was scheduled to fly to Springfield, Missouri, for the fall semester, he had not yet received his acceptance letter. However, the next day just before Mark and his father left for

the San Francisco airport, the letter from CBC arrived, welcoming
Mark as a member of the freshman class. Mark was on his way to
college and to play for the *Revivaltime* broadcast.

After completing two years at CBC, Mark was offered a part-
time position as minister of music at Calvary Community Church
in San Bruno, California. During that time he attended Simpson
Bible College in San Francisco (now Simpson University in
Redding, California). Mark's musical ministry had taken off!

With an intense desire to graduate "on time" with his B.A.
degree in humanities with a concentration in music, Mark
decided to transfer to Southern California College (now Vanguard
University) in Costa Mesa for his senior year. Both Dr. J. Calvin
Holsinger and Dr. John Leverett worked carefully with Mark in
the transfer of credits, and he graduated with the class of 1972.
With the supervision of Dr. Waymann Carlson, Mark did his
student teaching at Ensign Middle School and Newport Harbor
High School and then enrolled in a Master's program at California
State University, Long Beach. During this time he taught music
part time at Westminster Christian Schools at Christ Church of
Westminster.

In 1972, he also began working at Southern California College
(SCC) as organ accompanist for the College Choir conducted by
Professor Laszlo Lak. With orchestra, they performed such works
as Handel's *Messiah,* Haydn's *Creation*, and Dubois' *Seven Last
Words of Christ.* These were also performed in local churches and
on live television. A few years later, Mark assisted the chair of the
music department, Professor Edwin Elliott, with administrative
duties and curriculum revisions. Mark also taught music classes
then, in addition to having private organ and piano students, and
was organist for Stainer's *Crucifixion.* In 1973, versatile Mark
organized a mixed trio to represent SCC at the General Council of
the Assemblies of God in Miami Beach, Florida. Mark received his
Master's degree in music in 1974. What a man with a mission!

When Mark accepted a position at Garden Grove Community
Church in 1976, he continued at SCC in a part-time capacity.

With the completion of the Crystal Cathedral in September 1980, his ministry there demanded more time, so he was unable to continue at SCC. For eighteen years he remained at the Crystal Cathedral – playing for worship services, accompanying the choirs, performing for *The Glory of Christmas* and *The Glory of Easter*, assisting with literally hundreds of weddings and funerals, and being involved with many other musical responsibilities. Indeed, Mark had become the man with a musical mission!

Mark was never idle. He persevered and completed almost two-thirds of the course work for his doctoral degree in sacred music at the University of Southern California (USC) before the tragic accident in August 2003. He had received a half-tuition scholarship from USC for the 2003-2004 academic year, but he was not able to use it because he was still hospitalized in Maine when classes started.

Having known Mark since 1971, I have observed him as a student, professor, accompanist, worship leader from the organ, solo performer. Everything he does is with excellence! I remember being his guest many times when he played for *The Glory of Christmas*. He was permitted to have two guests sit by the organ console – and my husband and I were more often glued to watching Mark's feet as they swiftly swept over the pedals. How could a man play the organ with his feet and his hands? This is what flashed through my mind that day when the Vanguard University (VU) Alumni Office was informed that Mark had lost his left arm in a tragic automobile accident. My first words were, "It can't be true! He needs his arms and his feet." But even as I uttered those words, I knew in my heart that this man with a musical mission would somehow keep on playing for the glory of God. Just days before, I attended the *Revivaltime* reenactment program in Washington, D.C. I had shaken Mark's hand. We had embraced, and Mark had two arms. With this shocking news, I was in tears, but I knew there were alumni who would pray for the miracle that Mark still needed – that his life be spared! Daily, for weeks, I made calls to, and received calls from, concerned alumni.

It was March 21, 2004, when I traveled to Pasadena with VU President Murray Dempster and his wife, Coralie, to attend the Affirmation of Faith and Life benefit concert at Lake Avenue Church. It was so appropriate for Dr. Dempster, the president of Mark's alma mater, to lead in prayer. That night the entire congregation (over 3,000 people) was lifted into the heavenlies with the musical sound of the choirs and orchestra. An enthusiastic standing ovation was given to Mark when he performed at the mighty Casavant pipe organ.

Some weeks later, when Mark returned to his alma mater for a chapel service, he was interviewed by Carlos Fernandez, pastor of Worship Ministries. At the conclusion of the interview, Mark walked to the organ and played his signature piece, Toccata on "Hymn to Joy," after which the entire student body broke into spontaneous applause and a standing ovation. The man with a musical mission was a victorious testimony to the VU students, staff, faculty, and administration!

Everywhere he worked, Mark inspired those around him. His constant striving for perfection and excellence came shining through. During the twenty-four years that I was SCC/VU's alumni director, it was a delight for me to work with Mark on many alumni projects. I called him on numerous occasions to talk about creative ways of contacting alumni and for original ideas in promoting SCC/VU. I well remember one particular event when Mark suggested an alumni chapel service featuring four successive SCC presidents. In his unassuming, creative style, Mark said, "Let's call it the Presidents' Prayer and Praise Service" – and we did! There were so many luncheons when Mark and I would sit and discuss ways to grow the Alumni Association.

He served on the VU Alumni Board of Directors for three terms, both as a member and as treasurer. Most recently he fulfilled his position as president of the board. He helped to plan alumni fund-raising banquets over a number of years featuring Art Linkletter, and then Norma Zimmer, and then Tom Netherton and Rosey Grier. He dreamed of a world-class pipe organ for the proposed new VU Chapel and started the Pipe Organ Fund which is still ongoing.

In 1998, Dr. John Leverett invited Mark to return to VU where he again joined the faculty until 2002 as assistant professor of music. Mark's talent and ability came shining through as he played for the 100-voice University Concert Choir conducted by Dr. James Melton, which performed John Rutter's *Magnificat* on campus and at Carnegie Hall. During various years Mark was both Baccalaureate and Commencement organist at Vanguard. He also played for the annual Academic Convocation. Mark never missed an opportunity to minister in music and share his love of organ music in worship!

All through these years, Mark inspired his students as he taught piano and organ, as he taught in the classroom, as he encouraged them in various recitals, and as he performed for them. He made a piano CD entitled *Hymns of Faith*, which was sold at his concerts. For thirty-six years, I have watched Mark live by the words in those hymns of faith as he pursued his musical mission. All proceeds were directed to the Mark Thallander Endowed Organ Scholarship Fund at VU, which he established to help organ students. He also spearheaded the establishment of several other endowed music scholarships to assist students.

Mark's work extended to mentoring musical ministers. Hundreds have studied with him. He could hardly name them all. However, among them are public and private school music instructors, college professors, pastors, missionaries, musical theater directors, opera singers, ministers of music, church organists and pianists, presidents of music companies, adult choir directors, children's choir directors, and many other professionals.

In spite of the horrendous accident in August 2003, Mark's faith and determination came through just three months later. On November 15, at his father's memorial service, after I led in prayer, I watched as Inez Pope and Mark performed an organ duet, "Praise to the Lord, the Almighty." This man with a musical ministry was undefeated. And he will go on thrilling audiences with music for the glory of God!

One Year Later in Worcester

by Judith Hanlon

Immediately upon meeting Mark in 1968 when we were both seventeen and attending Bible college in Springfield, Missouri, I became a "Mark Groupee."

I listened to Mark rehearse at the piano and drooled. Because Mark was the accompanist for the Revivaltime Choir, I tried out for it. I didn't make it. I tried out for every choir on the campus (there were about six). I didn't make them either. Thus, to enjoy music, I had to be around Mark MORE! We went to a spring banquet together, yes on a date! I tried to break the Guinness world record for the number of college students squished into a phone booth. Mark was one of my guinea pigs for the world record. I am glad that he didn't suffocate. I was, of course, safely on the outside directing. These were a few of the youthful experiences that grounded a friendship that is still laughing, singing, and trying to do the impossible!

Mark went off to music fame and fortune, cavorting with the big names. I married and moved to New England. I heard about Mark often and wished that I could see him again. Central Bible College (CBC) published an alumni directory in which I discovered his e-mail address. We had great cyberspace chats. By now, I was divorced and pastoring a small New England Congregational church.

You know the story from here. During summer worship that combined four central Massachusetts congregations, our organist was on vacation. I called Mark, who was vacationing in Maine.

What you may not know is how much attention to the details and nuance of our worship Mark paid. He came down a night early with a binder of notations related to the service preparation we had discussed via e-mail. He had the bulletin marked. He had rehearsed accompaniment for special music. He rehearsed with our soloist and on the organ the Saturday night before. He asked about speed of congregational singing, segues, and more. I kept reminding him that we couldn't pay him what he was worth. You *know* that Mark just laughed about that. We went out for dinner and laughed as we remembered our younger days.

You are familiar with the story of the tragedy that followed that service on Sunday, August 3, 2003. I want to let you know that the worship that preceded that accident was grace filled and Spirit inspired. I remember one man who had always said to me, "I don't like too much music on Sunday morning." This particular Sunday he said, "I could have stayed for the entire day. Mark is incredible."

Then, the accident.

What you also may not know is that I was on vacation the minute that Mark left my house and headed through the rain toward Maine. Thus, I shut off my cell phone and began to pack for a trip home to visit family in Indiana.

Gary DeVaul did not have my home number, just my cell number. It wasn't until Tuesday night after the accident that Gary was able to reach me when my recharged phone was turned back on. When he told me that my dear friend Mark had been in a terrible accident and had lost his arm, I screamed. Screamed bloody murder, as they say. Delayed my trip . . . and cried the night away.

The following day, I drove to Maine to see Mark. I will never forget walking into that hospital room. I thought I would pass out from grief, horror, and sadness. I walked to the bed and looked at Mark, speechless. As only Mark can do, he weakly said to me, "How do you like my hair? Daniel, your parishioner, cut it."

I began to cry. "Mark," I said, "we have talked much about being single and living alone and going through scary times all by ourselves. I am just so sorry that you had to go through such a horrifying experience *alone*." Mark smiled up at me and said, "Oh Judy, I wasn't alone. Jesus was with me all the time."

I came to comfort Mark, and he ministered to me, both with his humor and his sweet faith. I placed cold cloths on his burning head and sang "Jesus Loves Me" to him. I knew nothing else to do.

The following year, Mark, with his indomitable spirit, wanted to do an anniversary service at the same church, on the same organ, with the SAME spirit of gratitude for life and for music. And so we did.

On August 1, 2004, Mark surrounded himself and the congregation with his talented musical friends. Some played one half of organ arrangements, with Mark playing the other half. Others provided the "surround sound" of music for worship. Jeremy McElroy, Julian Revie, Willie Sordillo, and Jon Clark. Four choirs, directed by Scott Yonker, sang "Come, Christians Join to Sing," a choral introit that Mark created specifically for this one-year anniversary service. The Prayer of Invocation was one that had been posted on Mark's CaringBridge Web site following the accident and one that encouraged him immensely in the darkest nights.

> *Giver of life, creator of all that is lovely,*
> *Teach me to sing the words to your song;*
> *I want to feel the music of living*
> *and not fear the sad songs*
> *but from them make new songs*
> *composed of both laughter and tears.*
> *Teach me to dance to the sounds of your world*
> *and your people,*
> *I want to move in rhythm with your plan,*
> *Help me to try to follow your leading*
> *To risk even falling*
> *To rise and keep trying*
> *Because you are leading the dance, Amen.*
> – anonymous

Tears and choked voices made it difficult to continue, but with Mark's great courage before us, we did.

I interviewed Mark during the worship service. He continued telling folks about God's presence and joy in his life. He told us that friends from all over the world were now rearranging organ music for one hand, two feet. He talked about an angel, a woman, who saved his life at the accident scene. He laughed through the tears, which begged that we laugh with him. Together with the congregation, we sang the old ones, "Great Is Thy Faithfulness," "Day By Day and With Each Passing Moment," and "Praise to the Lord, the Almighty." We joined in a corporate prayer of confession:

Dear Faithful One,
We confess our tendency to trust what we can see.
We confess that discussions of angels and
mystery and healing and hope, leave us yearning yet skeptical.
Break into the places where we are frightened and alone.
Break into the places where we are friendless and broken.

Invite us to believe again. Give us eyes to see the angels all around.
We wait silently now, for your visit, for your voice.

That missing arm, that missing limb was before us all the time. It was hard to take one's eyes off such a profound absence. Yet, the music, the joy, the laughter, and the honesty were so utterly uplifting smack-dab in the middle of this visual gaping hole. All of us remembered poignantly one year before when Mark played with both arms and hands. Many simply broke down and cried as the service went on.

You know that I never made it into any of the choirs at CBC, so in desperation over the years I formed my own choir and wrote my own songs. One of those songs, Mark told me, brought comfort during his time of rehabilitation. We sang that song, too.

I Know the Plans I Have for You
Words and Music by Judith Hanlon, copyright 2003
www.passagesmusic.com

"For I know the plans I have for you, says the Lord, plans to prosper you and not to harm you, plans to give you hope and a future." – Jeremiah 29:11, NIV

Oh, I know the plans I have for you,
I know them very well
They're plans for you to prosper
And harmlessly to dwell
For I planned these plans so long ago
You were a twinkle in my eye
So, why on earth would I let you down?
You're the apple of my eye!

When I called into creation
The stars, the sea, the sky
When I dearly loved each one of you
That I came to earth to die
When I walked the dusty Calvary Road
I had YOU on my mind
I wrote you clearly in my Script
And my future's great design

Sometimes, you just can't see, my child
Just around the bend
The glory that awaits you
In the blowin' of MY wind
So, stay the course, step by step
Holding tightly to my hand
I'll never, ever let you go
I'll guide you through this land

From "Amazing Grace" by a fetching sax to "Amazing Grace" arranged by Frederick Swann, from "Jesus Loves Me" sung a cappella to the Toccata (Symphony V) played by Julian Revie, from music written by Widor and Sanborn to music written by a "wannabe," the worship garnered the most distant genres of Christian music and the most disparate emotions of grief and joy.

As you must know, Mark named this service, A Celebration of Life. Four churches – Hadwen Park Congregational Church, First Congregational Church, Bethany Christian Fellowship, and Park Congregational Church – hosted the event.

I would be remiss and unfaithful if I didn't tell you that there are times when I wake in a cold sweat reliving the day of the accident. Wishing that I had NOT invited Mark to play. Wishing that I had told him to wait before leaving my house. Wishing that I had offered to drive up to Maine with him. Then, it occurs to me that Mark is not wasting his time with the past and that those thoughts of control and self-centered power are actually quite egocentric! Because of Mark's love of life and indomitable spirit, I usually end those commiserating times with a text that Mark often quotes: *THIS is the day that the Lord has made; let us rejoice and BE GLAD in it"* (Ps. 118:24 ESV).

Mark never accepted my passive-aggressive marriage proposals. However, he did accept the invitation to play at my wedding on November 10, 2006. And, once again, he brought his friends. Paul Bandy, Jeremy McElroy, Eric Dale Knapp. Willie brought his sax. Can you just imagine the music at that wedding! Oh yes, the groom, my wonderful husband, Glenn Richards, is also madly in love with Mark! Who isn't!

Sometimes, you just can't see, my child
Just around the bend
The glory that awaits you
In the blowin' of MY wind

So, stay the course, step by step
Holding tightly to my hand [just ONE hand, Mark!]
I'll never, ever let you go
I'll guide you through this land

We are staying the course. All of us caught in this cosmic journey of joy and pain. Waiting, with baited breath at what our loving God has for us, just around the bend, in the name of Jesus whom we follow.

The Man, the Friends, and the Glass House

by Alicia Steinhaus

It was a hot night in a glass house in Southern California, but it definitely was not quiet! Nor was it ordinary like most warm nights in Southern California.

The commute across Los Angeles from home to work and back again was belittled by a trek to Orange County over the supper hour. Anyone having traveled Interstate 5 from Los Angeles to Orange County at the supper hour on a Friday evening can testify that every inch of the pavement is covered by a slow, yet very driven, maniacal herd of cars making their way to the feeding trough at the other end. Pleasant it is not, predictable it is, and on this particular day, necessary it was.

Upon arrival near our destination, we scrambled for some semblance of nourishment to avoid the growlies. We settled for the epitome of Southern California fast food – Carl's Jr. (Hey, it beats Krispy Kreme for supper.)

Finally, after what seemed an eternity of blacktop, tires, metal, and raging testosterone, the glass house was right before us in all its immense glory. Just the sight of it is amazing, never mind the aural delight that awaited. The structure of metal and glass reaches into the heavens as if to touch the face of God, and reflects the light therein for miles around. It's an awesome sight, certainly at the top of the list of places to see in Orange County.

No sooner had we joined friends on the plaza but the aural delights started with a recital on the Arvella Schuller Carillon, audible to anyone in the near vicinity. This lasted for a good forty-five minutes and evidenced not only impeccable musical and technical ability, but hordes of sheer endurance for the grueling workout of the Carillon. Julian Revie and Rick Breitenbecher will not soon forget their Carillon Olympics and the gold medal they won!

The Carillon perfectly set the stage for the opening work of the Keyboard Benefit Concert, Vierne's Carillon de Westminster, most delightfully performed by J. Christopher Pardini on the magnificent Hazel Wright Organ and by none other than the wondrous Ken Medema improvising carillons on his synthesizer. In true Southern California regalia, the fountains of the Crystal Cathedral joined in on the final fanfare. It was truly extraordinary!

From that point on it was a veritable feast of delectable organ perfectly set off by extraordinary piano. The list of artists was most impressive. Joyce Jones was masterful with Sowerby's Pageant, demonstrating some of the most impressive foot work in existing organ literature. Peter Green escorted the listener into the lush sounds of Chopin's Ballade no. 4 in F Minor. John West demonstrated the delicacies in "Hazel's" range of capability with Saint-Saens' Andante Sostenuto from Symphonie 3. Jan Sanborn delighted us with three piano pieces on well-known hymns artfully scored by herself and Fred Bock. Once again, Joyce Jones treated us with the Improvisation on "Aka tombo," J. Christopher Pardini with none other than Diemer's "Battle Hymn of the Republic," and John West with his Fanfare on "Sine Nomine." To each of these, "Hazel" rose perfectly to the occasion even though the warm evening air was challenging.

A true revelry of music at the Crystal Cathedral would not be complete without Frederick Swann, Crystal Cathedral organist emeritus. We were all delighted with his Meditation on "Amazing Grace" and Festival Toccata on "St. Anne." No sooner had the thunderous applause quieted but it started up again as Mark Thallander and Jeremy McElroy took a seat at "Hazel" for Charles Callahan's "Evensong."

If the evening was not sufficiently emotionally charged, it quickly heated up as Mark played for us the world premiere of "Fanfare of Hope" by Callahan, taken from a Suite for One Hand and Two Feet, composed specifically for Mark. If there is any organist on the planet who could recover from a full-arm amputation and continue to play as wonderfully as before, it is Mark Thallander! We had a glimpse of this truth in March 2004 at the Affirmation of Faith and Life benefit at Lake Avenue Church, but this performance cemented it beautifully.

In a grand tribute to Mark, the master of improvisation Ken Medema sang about his dear friend, the accident, and how the Lord has used Mark so mightily in the midst of a seeming tragedy. What the world sees as tragedy, God has proven through Mark to be glorious triumph to His glory. Graciously sung by Ken, it was testimony to the great faithfulness of a loving God.

All good things must come to an end, and what better way to finish our glorious evening in a glass house in Southern California with a man and his friends than to hear four pianists, Peter Green, Jan Sanborn, Kemp Smeal, and Julian Revie; one organist, Fran Johnston; and a host of revelers exclaim:

> *Great is Thy faithfulness, O God My Father!*
> *There is no shadow of turning with Thee;*
> *Thou changest not, Thy compassions they fail not:*
> *As Thou hast been Thou forever wilt be.*
> *Great is Thy faithfulness,*
> *Great is Thy faithfulness,*
> *Morning by morning new mercies I see;*
> *All I have needed Thy hand hath provided —*
> *Great is Thy faithfulness, Lord, unto me![1]*

1. "Great Is Thy Faithfulness" by Thomas O. Chisholm
   Copyright 1923 Renewal 1951 by Hope Publishing Company
   Carol Stream, Illinois 60188 www.hopepublishing.com
   All rights reserved. Used by permission.

Participants in the benefit concert at the Crystal Cathedral included: (back row l-r) J. Christopher Pardini, Kemp Smeal, Frederick Swann, Ken Medema, John West, Jeremy McElroy, and Peter Green; (front row l-r) Jan Sanborn, Joyce Jones, Mark Thallander, and Frances Johnston.

Mark and his duet partner Jeremy McElroy

Jeremy McElroy (r) and Mark bow after their Crystal Cathedral organ duet on Mark's dear friend, "Hazel" (the Hazel Wright Organ).

Ken Medema responds with an improvised song about a glass house.

Liturgical Suite

by Pamela Decker

I first saw Mark Thallander at the 2004 National Convention of the American Guild of Organists. One evening during the convention, I walked into the exhibit hall and spotted Mark, and I noticed that something had happened to his left arm. While the audience was assembling for Frederick Swann's recital at the Crystal Cathedral a couple of days later, a man sitting near me told me about the accident that Mark had in August 2003. Just minutes later, Mark appeared and made a gracious introduction to Fred's recital. For me, there was something immediately remarkable about Mark's presence; without any previous acquaintance with him, I somehow felt I was in the presence of an exceptional person of unusual strength and spirit. After I returned to Tucson, I found his Web site and read almost all of it in one sitting. I can't think when I've ever had so much admiration for someone I'd never met. His Web site inspires both laughter and tears, and it leaves a lasting impression on the reader. I left the computer room, found my husband, and announced that I would write a piece for Mark.

I decided to do this project as a surprise for Mark. My thanks and great appreciation go to Frederick Swann as his role as consultant and confidant during the composition process. Fred provided information about Mark's interests, tastes, and preferences, including the suggestion he might prefer a work based upon hymn and/or chant material. Fred spoke about Mark's devotion to church music and indicated that a hymn-based piece would be appreciated.

On February 5, 2005, Mark led a workshop in Tucson, and the completed piece was presented to him as a gift at that time. On that occasion, I was finally able to meet Mark and to explain the project.

Liturgical Suite, with three brief movements for Lent, Easter, and Pentecost, is conceived so that it is equally appropriate for both church and concert use. Performers may choose to play this work as conceived – for right hand and pedal – but it is also possible to be performed using both hands.

A Review

by Frederick Swann

In a review of Liturgical Suite in the February 2006 issue of *The American Organist*, Frederick Swann writes: "History provides us with interesting accounts of why certain works were composed. One of the most familiar deals with the Ravel *Piano Concerto* for left hand. Recently, we've seen several organ works for right hand and pedal. These have been composed by friends and admirers of Mark Thallander in response to a horrific accident in August 2003 in which he suffered the loss of his left arm at the shoulder. Mark has made an extraordinary comeback and is again teaching and performing despite the challenges he faces. This most recent compositional homage is by the distinguished American organist/composer Pamela Decker, and is a welcome addition to the repertoire for all performers. . . . So ingenious is the writing that a listener will think three hands are being used instead of one!"

(Note: *Liturgical Suite* is published by Wayne Leupold Editions WL 610009.)

Excerpt reprinted by permission of The American Organist Magazine.

Founding the Foundation

by Lois Bock

There are momentous occasions in each of our lives that are indelibly engraved in our hearts and memories. We never forget the circumstances surrounding these events. Some are of pure joy:

...falling in love

...holding a newborn baby for the first time

...executing a job well

...performing with excellence

...knowing that we are in the presence of God!

Then there are times of great sadness such as grief and loss. I've had them. So have you!

Who will ever forget where they were, whom they were with, or how they heard the news that airplanes had flown into the twin towers of the World Trade Center on September 11, 2001. These images are permanently engraved in our minds and hearts.

August 4, 2003, was such a time for me. Not long after dawn while still dressed in my robe, I went downstairs to start the coffee. Suddenly the ringing of the telephone shattered the peaceful early morning hour. My friend Jan Sanborn greeted me and then quickly asked, "Lois, are you sitting down?" I said, "No, should I be?" When she answered in the affirmative, I pulled out a chair by the kitchen table and sat down to await whatever bad news I knew was coming. I told her to continue. "Mark Thallander was in a very serious automobile accident last night and is in critical condition." Then Jan told me the shocking news about the amputation of his left arm.

Feeling like I had been hit in the stomach, at the conclusion of Jan's phone call I hung up the phone and continued to sit at the table. While slowly digesting this bitter news, I talked with God, "Mark is a concert organist and needs both hands and arms to continue in his work." Then I added, "His passion is making music to honor and praise You. How could this happen?" Then the thought occurred to me – when Mark becomes fully aware of the severity of his injuries, Mark will choose to die.

But I was so wrong! The accident took his arm and what he thought would be his lifelong career. But it didn't take his spirit, his faith, his dreams, or his sense of humor. Those were and are intact.

When a tragedy happens to someone we love, it seems that an unseen thread of compassion and pain weaves us together – binding us in community. That's what happened to Mark's friends when he lost his arm. Because each shared in his loss, hundreds and hundreds of friends and family bonded...

...each felt helpless...

...each wanted to do the impossible...

...to fix the problem – to ease his pain...

An oft-repeated What can I do to help? was heard in conversations across the nation.

...Friends phoned friends, Did you hear about Mark Thallander?

...Love, concern, and pain for our mutual friend drew us together.

...Shedding common tears, we wept for and with him who wept (Rom. 12:15b).

Mark's life and future lay in the hands of the One who has always loved him. Those of us who watched from the sidelines have seen that even in the darkness of this tragedy, our Lord was Mark's comforter. It wasn't long before we saw God's plan for him.

Since the time of his accident, God has brought healing to the physical, visible wounds. A team of doctors and therapists stopped the initial hemorrhaging, stitched wounds, strengthened bones and muscles. But God's healing delved far deeper into every level of our friend's body, emotions, and spirit. The healing has also touched those whose lives touch Mark. We have witnessed that God never wastes an experience. Whether it be joyful or painful, He uses each as a building block to something far greater than we can ever imagine. God has taken the broken dreams and restored a life. Of course, scars and questions will always remain, but now these are cradled in the knowledge that God, who cares for Mark, is lovingly writing a new chapter in his life.

Previously you read the story of the Mark A. Thallander Trust that was established and the inspiring choral concert that was given to benefit Mark. In the warm afterglow of that evening, the committee gathered for a debriefing. Someone suggested that this concert should be repeated. Another person said, "That sounds like a great reason to establish a nonprofit foundation." And with that suggestion, Mark found a new dream and vision. The Mark Thallander Foundation was conceived, and within a few months an exciting new ministry was born.

In February 2005, our first Mark Thallander Foundation Festival was held at Lake Avenue Church in Pasadena, California. Then in February 2006, our festival moved to the Cathedral of Our Lady of the Angels in downtown Los Angeles at the invitation of Frank Brownstead, the cathedral's director of music. There were 1,000 singers, and with every one of the 3,500 seats taken, latecomers had to stand in the back or along the sides.

At both festivals, we told the audience that the offering would be the "seed money" to establish festivals in other cities and in other nations. In November 2006, we planted some of that seed money in Worcester, Massachusetts, when we held our first East Coast concert. Once again churches joined their voices to praise God. The donors' gifts have been the basis to enable the Foundation to magnify its objectives and amplify its music into other venues. The Foundation continues to grow. In February 2007 another festival touched the lives of the Southern California audience, which gathered once again at the Cathedral of Our Lady of the Angels.

Plans are being made for two more festivals on the East Coast in the fall of 2007 and for a tour with American choirs in Austria in 2009.

It is our desire to extend our hands and hearts across the chasm that divides churches by welcoming choirs from almost every denomination. Assemblies of God, Baptist, Bible Churches, Christian Reformed, Catholic, Congregational, Covenant, Episcopal, Lutheran, Presbyterian, Reformed, United Church of Christ, and United Methodist congregations have all participated. We have also welcomed children's, high school, college, and seminary choirs. The Board of Directors and Advisory Council come from Assemblies of God, Baptist, Congregational, Catholic, United Methodist, Presbyterian, Episcopal, Lutheran, and Covenant churches. Eric Dale Knapp, our gifted music director, is Lutheran, and our renowned Festival organist, Frederick Swann, is Episcopalian. Mark Thallander, our energetic, evangelical, ecumenical, entrepreneurial leader, was raised Assemblies of God but is now proudly claimed by almost every denomination. Together we have become a family of God.

Today, another thread binds us – common joy! We are excited that God, who is the creator of all that is beautiful, has once again shown His love and direction to Mark. From the ashes of a lost career, God has ignited a new spark of hope and purpose. More people will now hear Mark's story and music than he ever thought possible, and the words and music will linger in their hearts. What a privilege to "rejoice with those who rejoice" (Rom. 12:15a).

MISSION AND VISION

The Mark Thallander Foundation exists to enable individuals to experience growth in faith and community through the gift of music.

The vision of the Foundation is to affirm and inspire church musicians, choirs, clergy, and congregations through festivals, concerts, and seminars – in the Los Angeles area, across the nation, and around the world.

The Foundation seeks to unify the Christian community through dynamic choral and organ repertoire.

The Mark Thallander Foundation is led by a gifted Board of Directors: Paul Bundy, Lois Bock, Dr. Peter Green, Eric Dale Knapp, Jeremy McElroy, Julian Revie, Alicia Steinhaus, Jeff Steinhaus, Dr. Frederick Swann, and Mark Thallander.

Advisory Council: Leanne Cusimano, Ross Dixon, Marilyn Fontana, Rosemary Jackson, the Rev. Dr. David Leestma, Judy MacLeod, the Rev. Thomas Matrone, James A. Person, Bruce Rhodes, Barbara Todd, John West, and Bruce Wilkin.

The Board of Directors of the Mark Thallander Foundation: (back row l-r) Paul Bandy, Jeremy McElroy, Eric Dale Knapp, Julian Revie, and Dr. Peter Green; (front row l-r) Dr. Frederick Swann, Lois Bock, Mark Thallander, Alicia Steinhaus, and Jeffry Steinhaus.

Oh, Canada!

by Ross Dixon

July 2003. It was a hot, steamy evening in Ottawa, Canada. St. Paul's Presbyterian Church began to fill up for what was to be an outstanding evening of music and praise to our Lord – organ and piano solos and duets, and joyous congregational singing of favorite hymns. Little did anyone realize what would be happening in a few days to our guest musician, Mark Thallander.

This was Mark's third visit to St. Paul's and to our home in Ottawa. My wife, Heather, and I had been looking forward to having Mark with us again for a ten-day visit. When Mark was around, we always had lots of music, good conversation, and many laughs. In addition, chocolate desserts were in abundance as Heather brought out her most "chocolaty" recipes for Mark's visits.

The concert was an exciting event and, yes, a hot one, too, because of a lack of air conditioning. For many in attendance perhaps the highlight was the great congregational singing supported so skillfully by Mark at the organ and by Phyllis Deeks, our church choir director and pianist, at the piano. For others, though, the highlight might have been, as it was for me, the gorgeous performance on two grand pianos by Mark and Phyllis playing Bach's Concerto no. 1 in C Minor. What expression and precision these two excellent musicians were able to achieve working together. It was electrifying! "Playing in concert with Mark is simply a delight," commented Phyllis about the experience of playing several piano and organ duets with Mark that night. "His expressiveness, his musicianship, his joy, and his absolutely unpredictable wit are always present. With every phrase, there is sensitivity that is only acquired through experience, and not just musical experience, but that greatest of all teachers – life! I think that although it is said that it takes 10,000 hours of practice to become a skilled artist, that must be only a starting point. God's school teaches us so much more – the ability to translate those experiences into our soul's expression, and that, for any keyboard musician, pours from the fingertips onto the instrument and spills out to the listening audience. When two musicians are 'in sync,' they bring all of their combined knowledge and craft to one outpouring, and the sum of the parts truly becomes greater than the whole."

It was only a few days after Mark's visit that we heard of his tragic accident in the Eastern United States. A call from Jeremy McElroy announced the shocking news. My immediate reaction was to fly to Portland, Maine, to be of help, but this didn't seem to be wise as Mark was receiving excellent medical care and lots of personal support from Jeremy and his good friend, the Reverend Gary DeVaul. Mark was immediately put on St. Paul's prayer chain. Regular updates on his condition were passed on to many caring friends here in Ottawa. In the coming weeks we kept the members of our congregation informed of what was happening and encouraged them to go to the CaringBridge Web site for updates on Mark's condition and to send their best wishes.

July 2005. Once again it was a hot steamy evening in Ottawa! After a two-year absence, Mark was back for another wonderful concert at St. Paul's. While we knew Mark was a fighter, probably none of us anticipated the remarkable way in which he would rebuild his life, even to the extent of being back at our church to play the organ again. I'd promised Mark that we'd have an air-conditioned sanctuary when he came, but unfortunately budget restraints and other priorities took precedence over finishing the installation of air conditioning. Nevertheless, an amazing water-cooling system was temporarily installed by our church's property committee chairman to bring down the temperature. It worked (sort of) but also added much humidity to the air, creating a clammy atmosphere. The church was filled almost to capacity for this very special evening. A sensitively written article about Mark that appeared that day in Ottawa's leading newspaper, *The Citizen*, had no doubt helped to draw a capacity crowd. Mark was joined once again by Phyllis Deeks at the piano and by his friend Jeremy McElroy at a second piano. I had the pleasure of leading the great congregation in singing several well-known hymns. How exciting it was to hear these hundreds of voices lifted in praise to God, accompanied by the organ and pianos.

Prior to performing at St. Paul's Mark had visited the television studios of Crossroads Christian Communications near Toronto for an appearance on *100 Huntley Street,* a daily Christian television program broadcast across Canada. The invitation to be on the program came through one of their producers who had heard about Mark and wondered if he might be willing to appear and tell his story. When it was decided that Mark would come to Ottawa for a concert in July, plans were made for him to go first to Toronto for this television appearance. A Rodgers two-manual organ was brought into the main studio from the chapel for Mark to play several hymn selections including his signature arrangement, Toccata on "Hymn to Joy."

In addition to appearing on the morning show *100 Huntley Street* (which was rebroadcast three times that day), Mark ended up on a two-and-a-half-hour Christian middle-of-the-night live phone-in prayer program at Crossroads. The host, the Reverend Paul Willoughby, was an old friend from Revivaltime Choir days who worked at Crossroads and who had heard about Mark's pending visit. Mark admitted after the program that he had real concerns about sitting beside the host on camera for that length of time. All went well, though, as God gave Mark the needed strength to sit there and concentrate on the incoming calls. He was able to encourage many of those who called in and to make helpful comments along with the program's host. Needless to say, at 5 a.m. after appearing on those two television programs, Mark was ready for bed!

What a privilege it is to call Mark a friend and to enjoy his company whenever we can get together. He's always welcome in Ottawa. Heather is ready with new chocolate desserts to tempt him!

A Memorable Reunion

by John W. Kennedy

As organist Mark Thallander hit the opening chord of "The Sinner's Friend" at 6 Wednesday night at the Pepsi Center he thought back to what happened at 6 p.m. August 3, 2003 – two years ago to the day.

Then, after playing at the first "Revivaltime" re-enactment at the Washington, D.C., General Council, Thallander drove to Maine in a driving rainstorm. His car hydroplaned, crossed a ditch and went into oncoming traffic. In the wreck, Thallander's left arm was ripped out of its socket.

Although one of the leading organists in the world considered giving up music, he instead has learned how to play only with his right hand and both feet. Although he continues to undergo physical therapy at least twice a week, he continues to perform throughout the country.

"This is a pretty emotional day," Thallander said before Wednesday night's performance. "But I couldn't think of a better place to commemorate the accident's anniversary."

"Revivaltime" alumni gathered for a half-hour re-enactment of the radio program that ran from 1950 to 1994 "across the nation and around the world."

The assembled included Dan Betzer, who served as the program's speaker for its last 15 years; Cyril McLellan, who directed the choir for 41 years; and Lee Shultz, narrator for a quarter century. Fifty-five choir members sang such old-time hymns as "Standing on the Promises," "Blessed Assurance," "Leaning on the Everlasting Arms" and the "Revivaltime" trademark, "All Hail the Power."

"There's a lot of respect and desire for the music of 'Revivaltime' again," McLellan said. "Many people would like to see it reintroduced in Assemblies of God churches."

Wayne Warner, retiring director of the Flower Pentecostal Heritage Center, initiated the idea for an on-site re-enactment, as he did with the first reunion concert in 2003.

Fountains of Friendship

by Stephen McWhorter

In the fall of 1978 I accepted the call of the Vestry of St. Paul's Church in Walnut Creek, California, to be their rector. An East Bay suburb of San Francisco, Walnut Creek was then experiencing tremendous growth. A great deal of the growth was due to the expansion of the BART rapid transit system from San Francisco to that area. The parish I came to serve was stable and had enjoyed long-term pastorates. However, there was not a strong commitment to grow the faith community. My first year there proved to be a very short honeymoon because my energy level and vision were high and I was more than proactive about challenging the community to move forward. Resistance of all kinds was present, and the challenge to lead became quite frustrating.

My inability to motivate drove me to watch religious television, including Robert Schuller's *Hour of Power*. In one of the broadcasts Dr. Schuller talked about a conference for pastors called the Institute for Successful Church Leadership. Frankly I had never heard all of those words used in the same sentence. I needed help, so I enrolled. Spending four days in Garden Grove, California, was the beginning of the renewal of my ministry and the beginning of a long friendship with Mark Thallander. While attending the conference I heard great music, hymns sung with enthusiasm and power, led by the great organs and accompanied by fountains, and the words of Ephesians chapter 4 come alive emphasizing that the task of leaders is to equip the lay people for the ministry of the church. That was a new beginning for me.

After the morning session one day I made my way to the organ loft and met Mark. I was impressed by his technical skill – and what a sense of humor. I explained to him that I was an Episcopal priest, and he said, "We are here to encourage everyone." That began a number of conversations with Mark and eventually with the Music Ministry staff at the Crystal Cathedral. I was impressed by their professionalism, commitment to the task, and extraordinary gift of humor. Spending time with Mark would encourage anyone to move forward in their ministry. I kept wondering what made him so positive, and then I began to understand more fully his commitment to our Lord and the desire to give God praise in his music.

In ongoing conversations, Mark gave me wise counsel about how to energize the music ministry at St. Paul's Church. That involved some changes in staff which were painful and traumatic. Yet in reflection those changes had to be made. One thing stood out for me in Mark's counsel, and that was his encouragement to make the music ministry position in our church full time. Having attended the conference and then beginning to apply the teaching bore fruit. I also began to realize that ministry in all of its forms is the work of all people. Mark encouraged me to take the ministry of the laity seriously and to compensate them appropriately. My experience of the church is how we have not cared well for staff, citing the issue that funding does not permit it. Frankly that attitude is not one of leading by faith but rather by fear. The work of the Institute and talking with Mark opened my eyes to see that God's work demands that we risk and we risk a great deal. The level of fear for me initially was great; however, the more I led by faith, the more I became aware of God's blessing of the work. Always the humor was there, as well as the nudge to think about doing it differently. When I think of applying this faith leadership style and the reaction of folks who heard me, I can now laugh and thank God I was called to lead in that way. The reality at the moment was not sometimes well received by those whom I was attempting to lead.

During the summers of 1983 to 1985 I was one of the supply pastors at the Crystal Cathedral asked to preach. Mark was there as well as Fred Swann, whom I admire greatly. During the convention of the Episcopal Church in Anaheim in 1985 I was the guest preacher and our choir from St. Paul's filled in for the music ministry at the Cathedral. Mark was the one who made this happen, and I appreciated his trust. That Sunday the convention center filled to capacity because the Archbishop of Canterbury was present. A significant overflow came to the Crystal Cathedral and I think were pleasantly surprised to see an Episcopal priest and choir leading worship. Mark smiled and said his church was a full-service institution, meeting the needs of all and especially the Episcopalian who came to worship.

After nine years of ministry in Walnut Creek and a three-year sabbatical on California's north coast, I came to Northern Virginia. During those years in California I would speak with Mark, and the theme was always a positive one of encouragement while subtly challenging me to use in all things the gifts God had given me. Those kinds of conversations make you smile and thank God for His generous spirit in bringing people into your life who bless you. In the spring of 1990 I accepted the call of the Bishop of Virginia, Peter James Lee, to plant a new faith community in Auburn, a suburb of Washington, D.C. Four families had been gathered by the Reverend Victoria Heard to study and pray about a new church in this area. They met for almost one year, and then the search began for a founding pastor. When I was asked and subsequently interviewed, my first impression was not positive. I think most of that was because I had not considered planting a new church as something I might do. What a surprise and joy God has given to me. When I thought I might spend time in ministry doing pulpit supply or part-time work, God was calling me to work in church planting. I remember a conversation with Mark who said, "Try it." He was right.

Easter 1990 ushered in our first worship service at St. David's, with sixty-one people in attendance in a tent on property which had been left to the diocese. It was pouring rain, and eleven cars got stuck in the mud. It was a wet beginning, but the next sixteen-plus years were the greatest blessing for me. It is much easier to plant a new church than to try to redefine or renew an existing congregation. So I took the skills I had learned in Garden Grove and used them with positive results. Mark echoed what George Gallup said in one of his books that the great churches are going to be built with solid teaching and music. So as we began St. David's, the first person I brought to staff was our music minister, Liz Rozenbroek. On Easter Sunday I put an ad in the *Washington Post* announcing the position, and Liz responded. Liz blessed us for nine years and grew a significant program. The counsel I had been given opened me up to equipping St. David's with a dynamic and caring lay staff that built the congregation.

In the first nine years we built three buildings including our award-winning church in which Mark has played, with fountains down the center aisle. When he has come to be with us, I have always asked Mark to share in a conversation during the message and then play for us. Mark was with us the summer of his accident and played beautifully. His interpretation and joy in leading the hymns of the church is so exciting. Consistent with every other conversation with Mark was always the care he gave to see how I was growing the music ministry. Solid advice given with such courtesy and yet real strength.

When Jeremy McElroy called me with the news of Mark's tragic accident, I grieved and wondered what will happen. I spoke with Mark in the hospital in Maine, and again he encouraged me in my ministry. There was little self-pity or focus on himself. He did remark how pastorally well cared for he was from the ministry team at the Cathedral Church of St. Luke in Portland. The sacramental life of the church I know was a blessing to Mark. Through a CaringBridge Web site established for Mark, I was able to connect and pray for him as we received frequent news about his recovery. Reading about his therapy at the rehabilitation hospital and opening the peanut butter jar made me laugh and know that

Mark was not about to stop making music. As his recovery began, I became aware in Mark's communications that God was preparing him for a new ministry.

He came back to St. David's to play for us. He spoke of the accident and gave clear testimony to the call of God on his life. As I write these words, I am humbled by what God can do in all of us. I am tearful now because as I listened to Mark I saw God at work and I felt renewed in my own ministry. Isn't it fabulous how God brings into your life people who, although you may not see them often, bless you? And recalling them in your mind brings a smile to your face and joy to your heart. Mark has that capacity.

On January 1, 2006, I retired after over sixteen years as the rector of St. David's Church. That was a Sunday, and I thought folks would enjoy celebrating with me and welcoming my successor Kevin Phillips that weekend. A great celebration was planned, and the attendance at worship and the lunch following was tremendous. One part of the program was not given to me. What I did not know was that Mark had been brought to St. David's to play for the service. Just before we began worship I was wandering through the church greeting people, and over in a corner so as not to be seen was Mark Thallander. I was again humbled by his presence, his music, his friendship and support. Wow, what a day!

Since retiring (or rather redeploying) after forty years of ministry, I have moved to Alabama. For ten months in 2006 I served as the interim rector of the Church of the Ascension in Birmingham. While there I invited Mark to come and play for us. What power God has given him in his music.

When I think about Mark, I think about a man with so many gifts who has dedicated all that he has to the risen Christ. Mark is a man about the work of the Lord. He is consistent, humorous, and faith filled. Thanks be to God.

Champions

by Gary DeVaul

It was June 20, 2002. My friend Linda and I were wandering through Windsor Castle in London for the first time since the fire that destroyed one-third of the building just a few years earlier. It was Queen Elizabeth's Golden Jubilee Celebration, honoring Her Majesty's fifty years on the throne. We were excited to walk through the heart of history and share in the festivities. We turned from the foyer and entered the grandest room in the kingdom. St. George's Hall spread before us. Our eyes were drawn from the bright banners of state to the new ceiling, which is covered with the coats of arms of all the great knights and heroes of days gone by. Then past the great windows that filled the room with light, to the eastern end of the hall. There, perched on a great balcony high above the monarch's throne, stood the king's champion on a horse, covered with shining silver armor, a gleaming sword in hand.

St. George, the dragon killer, is the patron saint of England and Russia as well. His legend is the stuff of ancient mythology. It's grounded in the story of the Archangel Michael in Revelation. Well, there he was, resplendent in his armor, his great charger proudly bearing him. He was covered with silver, gold, and precious stones. His gleaming sword proclaimed the champion of champions! The symbolism is powerful. My mind was drawn back to chapter 20 of the book of Revelation, where the heavenly host is in close battle with the dragon, Satan. Michael is beating and binding Satan in chains and throwing him into the pit for a thousand years. And then my mind turned to St. George, slaying his dragon, and our dragon, the dragon within, that hoards the gold it cannot spend and the maiden it cannot ravish. Wow, as Mark would say. It is powerful stuff, and it is part of our faith.

The word *champion* is derived from the Latin word *campio.* *Campio* translates "gladiator" and is also the root of the word *campus,* where the champions compete even today. The one element that the great statue of St. George is missing is blood. There are no physical scars of battle here in St. George's Hall. Yet every champion has scars somewhere. The Archbishop Fulton J. Sheen described the scars of Jesus as "the marks of love." A poet once described Jesus on the cross as "the uncaught captive of love." A bit romantic, you say? Yeah, I guess so. But it works for me.

The whole idea of the champion is a romantic notion. Frankly, the notion is lost today, and it is our loss. The champion bears his, or her, wounds with grace and even an element of pride; not pride in himself, or herself, but pride in the cause for which he or she battles. The champion is always the champion of another. A champion may be bloodied but never beaten. There is something sacred about champions and the scars they bear. When we relinquish the romantic for the purely rational, the bloom bleaches from the rose and we lose much more than the liver shiver of the moment. We lose the meaning as well. And what is the meaning carried in the breast of every champion? Sacrifice. And what is the root word in sacrifice? It is *Sakre,* or sacrament.

Our wounds can become powerful. Our scars can become sacred. They can call up healing powers to the forefront of our lives, or they can routinely destroy us. If we chose, I am convinced that our wounds offer us the opportunity to sacramentalize, or make sacred, that which would normally be mundane yet deadly. Wounds need not be physical. Wounds come to us in every shape and size. They need not be worn as braggadocios' badges of courage. Like St. George of legend, a real champion reveals the scars in his eyes and voice and backs them up with action.

My friend Ron and I were escorted into the little waiting room near the recovery area of the Trauma Center where Mark was lying. The young plastic surgeon came to us with a look in his red-rimmed eyes that betrayed a champion's sacrifice. He was an experienced young man, but not jaded. He deeply regretted what circumstances had forced upon him. Yet he was faithful to his calling to save. And save he did. He was a champion. You could see it in his eyes.

Sometimes you can recognize the voice of a champion. Mark asked me to call Officer Stubbs of the Maine State Police. He was the first officer on the scene after the crash. When I called to find out how to retrieve the accident report, Officer Stubbs said, "I heard that Mr. Thallander is a great organist. Is that true?" "Yes," I replied. The officer was quiet for a moment, and one could sense that something was coming. Then he spoke the words of a champion. "You tell Mr. Thallander that if he's really great, I mean as great as they say that he is, he will play again." It takes a champion to know a champion, and Officer Stubbs dragged one from a green 4Runner that night. In his own way he was calling Mark back. Back to the greatness that is his. Officer Stubbs was a champion. You could hear it in his voice.

Some of us think that we don't have what it takes to be champions because we suffer fear. Champions are brave, but one cannot truly be brave unless one is truly frightened. We have a Champion who faced scars, and torture, and humiliation. He prayed in the garden and trembled with fear as the Author of Life faced death. His comrades neglected Him and slept the heinous hours away. Three times He begged His Father to spare Him the cup. In that litany of three prayers we are saved. For He drank the cup for a greater cause than He measured in His own skin, and He saved the sleeping, tardy knights on the garden floor – and us as well. He taught us that dark night in Gethsemane that our courage need only outweigh our fear by a drop of blood and one ounce of faith and we, too, become champions. He is our Champion because He acted. He took up the cross, and the cross became His sword.

We have an opportunity to relearn and recapture the precious lesson taught in the garden and on the cross. In His last words Jesus said, "Father, into Your hands I commit My spirit." In those last words found in Luke 23:46, our Champion gives over His scars, His wounds, His pain, the very sting of death. He "sacramentalized" the moment by giving it to God, and resurrection became His lot. We can do the same thing with our wounds. We, too, can consecrate our sorrow and grief. The injustices done, the abuse received, the insults felt, the anger and psychological pain endured. In doing so, we, too, can live the life of the Champion.

There was another champion in the hospital that dark and rainy night. His horse was a gurney. He was dazed but not beaten. I saw it in his eyes and heard it in his voice. There was blood in his hair and on his face. Yet calm acceptance claimed his heart. The brutality done him could not measure up to the faith within him. There was in that recovery room a sacred prayer-like quality that harkened back to Gethsemane, where Jesus prepared Himself for battle. When the carnage of the night was confirmed, Mark said, "Oh, wow," and closed his eyes. Behind those eyes, he put on his helmet, strapped on his armor, and in his strong right hand there appeared the champion's gleaming sword.

There is one more essential concept related to champions. They are often prone to hang out together. They have their fraternity, their round tables, be they in Camelot, in Windsor, on Web sites, or in the Upper Room. They tend to gather and support one another's cause – champions all for One.

> *Ever singing, march we onward,*
> *Victors in the midst of strife;*
> *Joyful music leads us sunward*
> *In the triumph song of life!*[1]

1. "Joyful, Joyful, We Adore Thee" by Henry van Dyke.

Appendix A

In Loving Memory

by Mark Thallander

"Blessed are the dead who die in the Lord . . .
they will rest from their labor, for their deeds will follow them."
– Revelation 14:13 (NIV)

This special section is devoted to sharing about the lives of three of the most important people in my life. In the next few pages, you will find information about the memorial services of my parents and Gary DeVaul. If you did not know them, you will get to know them after reading the tributes presented at their services.

Wilfred Lasse Emmanuel Thallander
January 9, 1912-August 10, 2003

The Lord called my father home just one week after my automobile accident in Maine. Because of my own hospitalization, I was not able to be physically present at the funeral service in Lodi, California, on August 13, 2003, so our family planned a Celebration of Life later when I could attend and participate.

Friday, December 5, 2003 (posted by John West on Mark Thallander's CaringBridge Web site)

It was an early morning rising – 5 a.m. on Saturday, November 15. On Sunday, on Easter, once a year . . . that's one thing. On an overcast Saturday in November . . . all I can say is it took the love of a good friend to get me to do that.

I arrived at the airport bleary eyed thinking I was late. But typical of my 'not' favorite airline, they were late, so I was fine. Minding my own business and chomping on a scone from Storybooks, I was approached from behind and tapped on the shoulder. There were Bill [Wells] and Craig [McKnight] who were also going to the celebratory event, with Bill actually participating. So I immediately woke up as the joy of good conversation will do to one. Finally we departed 20 minutes late and having to change gates [ahh, typical] but had an uneventful trip to "The Terminator's" new home city, Sacramento.

We were met by our host for the day, Steve Brenizer, who drove us to Stockton. Steve is principal at one of the largest elementary schools in Elk Grove [California], a friend of Mark's from Vanguard [University], and an all-around good person. He packed all of us over six-foot guys into his car, and we headed to Stockton.

Upon our arrival at the church I immediately set to practicing, since it was an unfamiliar organ and I was the final performer on the program. A lot of activity as preparations were made for the service. Choir slowly drifting in, the director warming up, sound and video cues going over, and Mark moving around easily, already dressed in his familiar suit and tie. Finally the appointed time came and the service began.

The Celebration of Life opened with Joy Baer playing a half-hour organ prelude of Wilfred's favorite hymns. That's right, a full 30 minutes of hymns and gospel songs he loved. As all of us organists know, sometimes 10 minutes can be very long! This was seamlessly woven into the Call to Worship in which the congregation stood and sang the powerful refrain to the Swedish tune "How Great Thou Art." Senior Pastor Jim Dunn welcomed everyone with gusto and let it be known from the beginning that this was a celebration and not a mournful event. And all the music represented that. The next hymn, "Joyful, Joyful," was sung with power and energy, followed by the Responsive Reading led by long-time Crystal Cathedral friend Nadine Breneman. Next the congregation sang the Hymn of Praise "All Hail the Power," which lifted everyone in the room and was followed by the Prayer of Praise powerfully delivered by Rosemary Jackson, special assistant to the president for alumni relations from Vanguard.

Without missing a beat the First Baptist Church Choir, under the direction of Stephen Olson, launched into the glorious anthem, "The Majesty and Glory of Your Name" and sang it with gusto. This was followed by a lovely, more peaceful time as Christy Pryor [daughter of Joyce, a niece of Uncle "Lasse"] spoke to the memories [see next article] she had with a video presentation behind her created by Wayne, Mark's brother. Long-time friend Linda Rust from Century Assembly in Lodi, accompanied by one of Mark's first musical influences, Linda Hauger [from Lincoln Neighborhood Church], then led the congregation through the old-time gospel hour with the Swedish songs "Children of the Heavenly Father," "He The Pearly Gates Will Open," and "Day By Day," with the congregation joining in on the last verse. Thought I was back at one of the prayer meetings of First Baptist Church Van Nuys!! Memory lane, ahh, memory lane.

Coming all the way from Newport Beach, William Wells, minister of music at Newport Harbor Lutheran Church, then led us in a stirring Prayer of Thanksgiving. This wonderfully led into the organ duet of Mark Thallander and Inez Pope, organist of Central United Methodist Church in Stockton. They were assisted by Brenda Martins, organist/choirmaster of St. John's Episcopal Church in Stockton. This has to be the high point of the service. The applause went on and on and, had it been a concert, surely a standing ovation would have spontaneously happened. It was the first time Mark had performed in public [since his accident], and it was a fitting tribute to his father and mother. To welcome the pastor for the Words of Hope, the choir did a new arrangement of Psalm 23 which was filled with eclectic rhythms and energy.

Senior Pastor Jim Dunn delivered his message eloquently. As he began, he commented on the fact that he probably would not stay in the time limit that had been assigned. But untrue to his comment, his words were brief, and true to his spirit, very meaningful. This was followed by a violin solo of "The Holy City" played very emotionally and beautifully by Stephen Olson, the pastor of worship and arts. The choir joined in the last refrain and made it another celebratory, uplifting moment. This was followed by the congregation singing the glorious hymn "For All the Saints" and David Leestma, executive pastor and minister of worship at First Covenant Church of Oakland, delivering the farewell benediction. And finally with very cold fingers I ended the service with the Postlude Fanfare on "Sine Nomine" ("For All the Saints") which Mark requested I play. This is an arrangement I have recorded, is published by Augsburg Fortress Publishers, and has been one of Mark's favorites. I was honored to be asked and obliged.

Following the service we all adjourned to the Welcome Center for the reception, which went on for a couple of hours and was organized by "Uncle Lasse's" nieces Diane and Karen. Finally around 6:00 we headed back to Sacramento to catch our flight home, so that both Bill and I could get up at the crack of dawn the next day to get to our respective church positions.

It was a gloomy day weather-wise, with light rain in the San Joaquin Valley, but it was a sunny day experience we had. All were blessed by the event, and all were witness to the life that brought together many peoples from differing denominations. Mae was in her glory and filled with a loving energy I finally had the opportunity to experience. Wayne and Mark were both joyful and tearful and never without a kind word for every person in attendance from near and far. Family pictures were taken and glorious desserts were consumed.

All I can say is it was a love-filled day and "You should've been there"!!

Uncle "Lasse"
Written by Joyce Pryor and read by her daughter, Christy Pryor

The word *servant* describes Uncle Lasse, not just for his family, but for anyone who was privileged to know him. He served his country, his family, his friends, but most of all his Lord. Uncle Lasse's relationship with the Lord helped him have a servant's heart just like Jesus. While we didn't grow up in Bible days with dusty roads and sandals, Uncle Lasse performed the modern version of washing feet – he polished his family's shoes.

Our family remembers that Uncle Lasse would polish Mark and Wayne's shoes and then his own. This is one of the many ways Uncle Lasse demonstrated serving his family. It is interesting, but not surprising to notice that Uncle Lasse's two sons chose careers in serving others. Mark serves in music ministry; Wayne serves by teaching and coaching. Their mother, Auntie Mae, also demonstrated serving in their home. If you ever visited their home, you were probably handed a home-baked snack and beverage the minute you arrived! Uncle Lasse's father must have influenced him in the servant's role as he was a cobbler and made shoes for others. Revelation 14:13 truly reflects the legacy of servanthood Lasse's father passed on to him and then on to his [Lasse's] sons. It says, "Blessed are the dead who die in the Lord . . . for their deeds will follow them" (NIV).

Another word to describe Uncle Lasse is giving. He gave time to his family, friends, and neighbors. He honored others above himself. Even when his arthritis made it difficult for him to walk, you could see him carrying a lawn chair or picnic basket at a family picnic to lighten another's load. For many years our family had a reunion at Micke Grove Park in Lodi. Uncle Lasse and Uncle Norm would get up early, get a thermos of coffee, and sit on picnic tables to reserve them. They gave of their time so everyone else could travel to the park and have the best tables in the shadiest location. Now my Uncle Lasse is saving a table in heaven for us, along with my Papa Art and Uncle Norm.

Psalm 37:23 tells us: "The steps of a man are established by the Lord; and He delights in his way." No one can ever fill Uncle Lasse's shoes, but they can serve as a reminder of the servant's heart we desire in serving the Lord.

Gary DeVaul
June 29, 1946-February 26, 2006

Getting Through It & More!
by Gary DeVaul

This was to have been the foreword for the new book which Gary and I were planning to write. Gary crafted this in January 2006, one month before the Lord took him home.

"I can't believe this happened to both of you after all you've been through together!"

Mark Thallander and I have both had that said to us a hundred times! Somehow, for some reason, people assume that we live in a fair world. For the most part, we all want to believe the best and think that two people who attempt to do good things for others shouldn't suffer. Well, sorry folks, but that's not the planet we live on. It would be nice if things were fair. Especially for the good guys, right? Well, think again. How does it go? God never said it would be fair, only that He would be there. Well, we found out that God was there, is there, will always be there. Incognito at times? Yep! But there, nevertheless. It has been quite a ride, and it's not over yet. So while it is fresh in our minds, we thought we'd tell you how we got through it thus far, and maybe it will help us make it a bit farther and a bit better. Maybe even help you and yours through your stuff, too.

We have known each other through most of our adult lives. Worked together, certainly played together. Mark and I have tons in common, everything from our relationship with Jesus Christ down to our love of music and affection for the church. Yet, you can ask anyone who knows us personally; we are really very different people. One of us hangs his shirts by order of color. One of us can't find his socks. One of us loves to cook. The other one might as well store church music in his oven. One of us is careful and mindful of details. The other one wouldn't know a detail if it hit him in the face. And so it goes. We are different. We suffer differently. Grieve differently, and triumph differently. But we both triumph, and how that happens is what Mark and I want to share with you.

Now don't get us wrong. We don't think we have cornered the market and have all the answers. We're not sure in every instance how we've come as far as we've come. In our own ways Mark and I have each enjoyed a special dispensation of grace that has made our lives bearable and downright livable. And we are both very thankful to our Lord for making that possible, especially under the circumstances. Loosing an arm could be considered a shock to one's system. Chemotherapy just wipes out one's system altogether. But none of it, nor all of it put together, is any match for the Man on the cross.

Postscript from Mark: It was the morning of Sunday, February 26, 2006 – the long-awaited day of our Mark Thallander Foundation Festival at the new Cathedral of Our Lady of the Angels in Los Angeles. Gary had flown in from Maine a few days before and was scheduled to give the prayer of blessing at the afternoon dinner, followed by a book signing in the Cathedral Gift Shop, and then offer the opening prayer that evening in the Cathedral. His youngest son, Phil, called me on Sunday morning as I was getting ready for church and left a message for me to call him. Phil told me that he was taking Gary to the hospital as Gary had been coughing all night. Within the hour, I received another message from Phil. I thought my cell phone had not erased the previous message, but just to be safe, I called Phil again. The second time I talked with Phil, he tearfully gave me the shocking news that Gary had collapsed in the bathroom, getting ready to go to the hospital, and died.

The following Saturday, a beautiful memorial service was held at the Crystal Cathedral in Garden Grove, California. Many people who had known Gary as pastor were in attendance. Two of Gary's favorite soloists sang two of Gary's favorite songs: Darlene Feit, "His Eye Is on the Sparrow," and Fred Frank, "Fill the World with Love" (Fred had sung this selection at Gary's ordination service in that same room in the late 1970s). Cellist Steve Velez, organist Richard Unfried, and I also participated.

Then in Ogunquit, Maine, a second memorial service was held on May 20, 2006. Eric Dale Knapp conducted a combined choir representing singers from five churches. Jeremy McElroy played one of Gary's favorite piano works, a Brahms' Intermezzo. Jeremy and I played Gary's favorite piano/organ duet, "Crown Him with Many Crowns," arranged by Bill Fasig and John Innes. The combined choir sang the introit "Come, Christians, Join to Sing," which I arranged, and "Like a River Glorious" by Dan Miller. The congregation "lifted the roof" of the Ogunquit Baptist Church with "All Creatures of Our God and King" and "Crown Him with Many Crowns." The service concluded with Albert Melton of St.

Luke's Cathedral in Portland, Maine, playing Gary's favorite organ work, Toccata (Symphony V) by Charles Marie Widor. Leanne Cusimano, owner of Amore Breakfast in Ogunquit and a dear friend, shared the following special tribute to Gary.

The Table
by Leanne Cusimano

Thanks for being here to honor the life of Gary DeVaul. I had the privilege to be in attendance at Gary's California memorial service in the Arboretum on the great campus of the Crystal Cathedral. What an awe-inspiring setting, filled with Gary's family and friends. Some of those friends knew Gary for twenty-five or thirty years. Although I knew Gary for just a fraction of that time, I left that experience so complete, knowing that I knew that "same" Gary those dear friends and family spoke of – the man who could so easily and sincerely say "I love you" at the end of a visit or phone call. He loved and accepted each and everyone one of us for being exactly who we are.

There are some people you meet who take forever to get to know, but not with Gary. He let you in, all the way, from the start. When we first met, he was a customer of mine when Cafe Amore was located in Perkins Cove, Maine, in the late '90s. He sat around a table surrounded by friends. One of the great benefits of the restaurant business is the opportunity to create real and lasting friendships. We welcome you in with outstretched arms, and the likes of Gary walk in and make themselves at home. Each time around the table Gary sat with new friends or family. I realized rather quickly that this man had quite an expansive circle, and he made it a point to introduce everyone to me – another bonus, more special friends for me!

Around that table, whether it was at his home, another restaurant, or the Village Food Market, friendships grew stronger, stories were shared, problems were solved, and great debates would take place. I sure hope that God is a Democrat, so the debates can continue! And boy, he could gossip like a woman in curlers under the dryer at the beauty salon! The many charms of Gary DeVaul.

While recovering at Gary's home, Mark Thallander experienced his first time out to eat at Amore after his accident. Around that table with Mark sat Gary and yet more friends who came to share love and support.

Gary didn't have much of an appetite while undergoing treatment for multiple myeloma. He didn't spend much time around the table. Weak and hurting, he suffered so, but when he regained his strength and found his appetite again, he was back at one of my tables, a little shorter and a lot crankier, with seat cushion in hand, enjoying the company of his beloved friends. Soon he was back to his regular routine, coming in to eat several times a week. It was always a delight to me to discover who would be joining in around that table.

Gary and Mark were my first visitors at my new home in January 2006. Gary tried to talk me out of entertaining them just hours after my moving crew had left, but Mark was flying home the next day and I was anxious to share my new surroundings with them. I was excited in the hopes that Gary, who lived just minutes up the road, would spend time around my dining room table in the future, surrounded by friends. We had a great visit, with Gary telling his stories and all the while Mark denying ever taking part in the escapades being described! We then went out for a bite to eat and found ourselves around a table, together for the last time.

I wish to thank Gary's sons for allowing me to share. Your dad was a cherished friend, and I loved him as he loved me. I am so grateful for the gift of one of Gary's favorite paintings which now hangs on my dining room wall, because while we are around that table, your dad will be remembered.

Mae Bernice Branvold Thallander
May 27, 1915-July 26, 2006

**7/26/2006 5:14:08 AM (posted by Mark Thallander on www.
markthallander.com)**

Now thank we all our God with heart and hands and voices,
Who wondrous things has done, in whom God's world rejoices;
Who from our mothers' arms, has blessed us on our way
With countless gifts of love, and still is ours today.[1]

After saying our Tuesday evening good-byes to our mother, my brother Wayne and I, along with my mother's sister Delores, were called by one of the caring nurses at St. Joseph's Medical Center here in Stockton. She suggested we return as quickly as possible. At 2:58 a.m. this morning (Wednesday) the angels arrived and escorted our mother into the presence of Jesus. Her last moments were so peaceful, and even though I was holding her hand, I had to put my ear to her mouth to realize she had stopped breathing. I told her moments later that she had taught us how to live . . . and now she had taught us how to die.

Thank you for your continued prayers for our family and friends. Thanks to Dodie, Jim, Joanne, Grace, DeAnna, Amy, Nadine, Dorothy, Inez, Pastor Kraft, Pastor Doug, and others, who came to visit today . . . and thank you for all of the phone calls. Our comfort is that Mom is in heaven, and we are rejoicing that Mom has been reunited with Dad. We know that she missed him very much. And what a welcoming committee she must have had.

Since she died in a Catholic hospital, I took the authority at 3:58 a.m. . . . just one hour after her passing . . . to pronounce her a saint.

Mae Thallander, a devoted follower of Christ, has received her crown . . . and just before she left us, I told her that Jesus was ready to welcome her and He would say, "Mae Bernice Branvold Thallander, well done, my good and faithful servant. Enter into the joy of your Lord!"

I sang many songs to her in the final hours, including this stanza of "My Jesus, I Love Thee":

In mansions of glory and endless delight,
I'll ever adore Thee in heaven so bright.
I'll sing with the glittering crown on my brow,
If ever I loved Thee, my Jesus, 'tis now.[2]

A few weeks ago Mom told me she needed her left arm [which had been affected by a stroke]. I told her I knew how she felt! Tonight I was able to tell her that she would have a new body . . . and that I was absolutely positive that the left arm would work!

What an honor and a privilege it was to be with her. I thank God for giving me this beautiful opportunity to minister to her until she was safe in the arms of Jesus.

This is the day that God has made . . .

We will rejoice and be HAPPY [Mom's version] in it!

Evergreen Chapel
by Mark Thallander

I had never been to Evergreen Chapel in Lodi, California. My father's funeral was there, but, as you know, I was unable to attend. For his funeral, several organ selections were played from my CDs, but for my mother's funeral, I was privileged to play the organ live in the Evergreen Chapel. I began the service with two hymn arrangements by friends of mine: "Great Is Thy Faithfulness" by Dan Miller and "Praise God, from Whom All Blessings Flow" by Fred Bock. Pastor Eugene Kraft, a dear friend of the family, assisted by Pastor Doug Butler, began the service with Scripture readings and prayer. The chapel was filled with family and friends who joined together in singing one of my mother's favorite hymns, "All Hail the Power of Jesus' Name."

All hail the power of Jesus name! Let angels prostrate fall;
Bring forth the royal diadem, and crown Him Lord of all;
Bring forth the royal diadem, and crown Him Lord of all!

Let every kindred, every tribe on this terrestrial ball,
To Him all majesty ascribe, and crown Him Lord of all;
To Him all majesty ascribe, and crown Him Lord of all!

O that with yonder sacred throng we at His feet may fall!
We'll join the everlasting song, and crown Him Lord of all!
We'll join the everlasting song, and crown Him Lord of all![3]

Several of my mother's friends spoke eloquently about their special relationships with her: Dorothy Bloecher, representing the Calvary Tabernacle years; Linda Hauger, the Lincoln Neighborhood Church years; and Nadine Breneman, the Crystal Cathedral and First Baptist Church years. Interspersed with the speaking I played Frederick Swann's setting of "Amazing Grace" and then accompanied Joyce Kraft as she sang my mother's favorite hymn, "Close to Thee."

Thou, my everlasting portion, more than friend or life to me,
All along my pilgrim journey, Savior, let me walk with Thee.
Close to Thee, close to Thee, close to Thee, close to Thee;
All along my pilgrim journey, Savior, let me walk with Thee.

Not for ease or worldly pleasure, nor for fame my prayer shall be;
Gladly will I toil and suffer, only let me walk with Thee.
Close to Thee, close to Thee, close to Thee, close to Thee;
Gladly will I toil and suffer, only let me walk with Thee.

Lead me through the vale of shadows, bear me o'er life's fitful sea;
Then the gate of life eternal may I enter, Lord, with Thee.
Close to Thee, close to Thee, close to Thee, close to Thee;
Then the gate of life eternal may I enter, Lord, with Thee.[4]

This concluded my portion of the service as the organist, and I was then able to sit with my brother, Wayne, and my Aunt Dodie. Just prior to Pastor Kraft's message, "Words of Hope," my cousin Diane and my cousin Karen's daughter Jill shared about their love for our dear mother (see the following article, "Auntie Mae").

With Mother and the funeral directors leading the procession, we followed them to the graveside ceremony, while Inez Pope played the Widor Toccata. After the closing words of committal by the pastors, we sang together another of Mom's favorite gospel songs, "Blessed Assurance."

> *Blessed assurance, Jesus is mine!*
> *O what a foretaste of glory divine!*
> *Heir of salvation, purchase of God,*
> *Born of His spirit, washed in His blood.*
> *This is my story, this is my song,*
> *Praising my Savior all the day long;*
> *This is my story, this is my song,*
> *Praising my Savior all the day long.*
>
> *Perfect submission, all is at rest,*
> *I in my Savior am happy and blest;*
> *Watching and waiting, looking above,*
> *Filled with His goodness, lost in His love.*
> *This is my story, this is my song,*
> *Praising my Savior all the day long;*
> *This is my story, this is my song,*
> *Praising my Savior all the day long.*[5]

Prior to the service, each person was presented with a pink rose. Following the Benediction, most of the people placed their pink roses on the casket. What a beautiful site it was to watch the casket spray expand as the many lives Mom had touched said their final good-byes with a special touch of love.

We then journeyed to Lakeview Assembly of God where the Women's Ministries had prepared a lovely luncheon. Following the luncheon, as we were driving to my Aunt Dodie's home – another serendipity – relatives were calling each other on their cells phones as a Christian radio station was playing a piano solo, "Blessed

Assurance," and it was from my piano CD. I think Mom was smiling upon us!

Auntie Mae

The following was written by my cousin Diane Geisler and shared at my mother's funeral service.

I am Diane, Mae's niece, and I am representing her fifteen nieces and nephews from California, North Dakota, and other areas.

(Holding up a doily made by Auntie Mae.) Auntie Mae made hundreds of these doilies. *(Holding up crochet thread and hook.)* And this is her crochet hook and thread. To many of us, it's just thread and a piece of metal, but in Auntie Mae's capable hands, it's a beautiful work of art. Today, Jill [my cousin Karen Richesin's daughter] and I are attempting to knit together a quilt of memories of Auntie Mae.

In the Bible, Psalm 139:13-14 tells us: "For you created my inmost being; you knit me together in my mother's womb. I praise you because I am fearfully and wonderfully made; your works are wonderful, I know that full well" (NIV).

Another Scripture that reminds me of Auntie Mae is 1 Peter 4:9-10, which says: "Offer hospitality to one another without grumbling. Each one should use whatever gift he has received to serve others, faithfully administering God's grace in its various forms" (NIV).

Auntie Mae used her gift of hospitality to serve others. Anyone who entered her home was graciously welcomed with a delicious homemade treat and beverage. And she continued serving her guests when they came to visit her at Rio Las Palmas.

Auntie Mae and Uncle Lasse modeled and encouraged their sons, Mark and Wayne, to use their God-given gifts and talents to serve others. Mark still uses his gift of music and testimony to minister to others. Wayne uses his gift of teaching and photography to serve others.

Even though Auntie Mae was an excellent secretary and bookkeeper, she had childhood dreams of becoming a church musician and teacher. However, that was fulfilled through her sons, Mark and Wayne.

Auntie Mae used her talents of sewing and baking to serve others. She was always sewing something for someone, whether it was making quilts or potholders, or baking pies or cookies or making jelly to share with others. I think most of us here today have been the recipients of her homemade specialties.

A fond childhood memory my sister, Joyce, and I have is of Auntie Mae teaching us songs. One particular song she taught us was different than the usual "Jesus Loves the Little Children of the World." Auntie Mae taught us her version, which goes like this:

Jesus loves the little children,
All the children of the world.
Irish, Dutch, Chinese, and Jew,
And the little Norwegian, too.
Jesus loves the little children of the world.

Well, we never sang that one in Sunday school, but we will always remember Auntie Mae's special version!

The Scripture that best describes Auntie Mae is Proverbs 31:10-31, and Jill and I would like to read verses 25 through 31 (NIV):

She is clothed with strength and dignity;
she can laugh at the days to come.
She speaks with wisdom,
and faithful instruction is on her tongue.
She watches over the affairs of her household
and does not eat the bread of idleness.
Her children arise and call her blessed;
her husband also, and he praises her:

"Many women do noble things,
but you surpass them all."
Charm is deceptive, and beauty is fleeting;
but a woman who fears the Lord is to be praised.
Give her the reward she has earned,
and let her works bring her praise at the city gate.

Rose Cottage
by Mark Thallander

My mother was my best friend, and I miss her dearly. Through the years I had wondered what I would do without her. A few days after Mom's funeral I arrived in Ogunquit, Maine. Now Dad, Gary, and Mom were in heaven. I was invited to stay in a home called the Rose Cottage next door to where Gary had lived. I went upstairs to my room on August 3, 2006, three years to the day after my accident. The first thing I did was put a funeral program, with Mom's picture on it, on the dresser. And what did I find on the dresser? A bouquet of pink roses – Mom's favorite. And here I was in the Rose Cottage. Wow! I felt God's comforting presence in that room.

The next day I went to practice the organ at the Ogunquit Baptist Church. The hymnal was opened to the gospel song, "Does Jesus Care?" I had heard the song before, but it was the final stanza, which I did not know, that touched me deeply.

Does Jesus care when I've said good-bye
To the dearest on earth to me,
And my sad heart aches till it nearly breaks –
Is it aught to him? Does he see?
O yes, he cares – I know he cares!
His heart is touched by my grief;
When the days are weary,
The long nights dreary,
I know my Savior cares![6]

1. "Now Thank We all Our God" by Martin Rinkart, tr. Catherine Winkworth.
2. "My Jesus, I Love Thee" by William R. Featherstone.
3. "All Hail the Power of Jesus' Name" by Edward Perronet and John Rippon.
4. "Close to Thee" by Fanny J. Crosby.
5. "Blessed Assurance" by Fanny J. Crosby.
6. "Does Jesus Care?" by Frank J. Graeff.

Appendix B
God's Continued Faithfulness
by Mark Thallander

I was asked by the concert committee to write letters which appeared in the printed programs for the Choral Benefit Concert in 2004 and the first Foundation Festival in 2005. These letters not only share information about my personal journey, but also offer sincere thanks to people who were greatly involved in my healing process at that time. I share these letters again to remind us of God's continued faithfulness.

Affirmation of Faith and Life
March 21, 2004
Lake Avenue Church
Pasadena, California

Greeting from Mark Thallander

Dear Friends,

Thank you for joining with us in this monumental festival of music! I am truly humbled and honored that you are here this evening for this special event. I also express my grateful appreciation to Eric Knapp who conceived and created, and is conducting this benefit concert, and to Janelle Grose and her Lake Avenue Church staff for overseeing a myriad of important details. Additionally I would like to thank the nearly 1,000 musicians, and the individual directors, most of whom are dear friends of mine, for so generously offering their musical gifts in this afternoon's rehearsal and in this evening's presentation.

Few people may be aware that each day during my mother's pregnancy, she joined in prayer with the pianist at her church that the unborn child would become a church musician. That pianist, Mavis Thompson, told the story when I was a student at Central Bible College on a choir tour in Minnesota. It has been affirmed throughout my life that being a church musician is more than just a career opportunity. It is a divine calling from God. To embrace the call and accept the challenge has resulted in my life-long commitment in serving Christ through the gift of music.

My music ministry started in high school when I accompanied Youth for Christ rallies and the YFC Campus Life Singers in Stockton, California. Then as a college student in Springfield, Missouri, I was pianist for the international radio broadcast *Revivaltime*, heard weekly on the ABC radio network. I also served as a minister of music and/or organist during college years at three Assemblies of God churches in California: Calvary Community Church, San Bruno; Lincoln Neighborhood Church, Stockton; and Newport-Mesa Christian Center, Costa Mesa. My first pipe organ was at Grand Avenue Church (United Methodist), Santa Ana.

I began my first full-time church position when Don G. Fontana hired me at Garden Grove [Community] Church in 1976. There I met Gary DeVaul who is master of ceremonies tonight. I served there for 18 years, eventually as assistant director of music to Frederick Swann in the new Crystal Cathedral. I am so grateful to Fred, and also to many choir members for participating this evening. Following that tenure, I was associate minister of worship at Menlo Park Presbyterian Church. Christian Elliott, staff organist at Menlo Park, received the Mark Thallander Organ Scholarship when he was a student at Vanguard University, and tonight represents our friendship from both Menlo Park and Vanguard days. In July 1995 I received a call from the Ministry Council of Lake Avenue Church to become director of music and organist. When I first arrived at Lake, I had the privilege of ministering with Dan Bird who was the associate pastor of worship. I am delighted he is here this evening to direct one of his compositions. After Lake, I served as assistant professor of keyboard studies at Vanguard University for four years, where soprano Amy Barnhart studied both organ and piano with me. While at Vanguard, I was also organist and interim director at Glendale Presbyterian Church and currently serve as an adjunct professor at Glendale College. I am so pleased that both Glendale church and college choirs along with Peter Green are represented here tonight.

Another aspect of my ministry has been as a guest organist. One of the first ministers of music to extend an invitation was John Sutton, then serving at Calvary Temple, Denver, Colorado, and later at Valley Christian Center, Dublin, California, and La Jolla Presbyterian Church. John is here this evening with his choirs from both Azusa Pacific University and Lake Avenue Church. Hanan Yaqub included me as an organist for the General Assembly of the Presbyterian Church (USA), and she is here with her choir from Trinity United Presbyterian Church, Santa Ana. John West represents Bel Air Presbyterian Church; Jubilant Sykes, Grace Community Church; plus singers from other churches where I have been a guest organist: The Church of Our Saviour, San Gabriel; First Presbyterian Church, Hollywood; Westminster Presbyterian Church, Westlake Village; First Covenant Church, Oakland; Saint Paul's Presbyterian Church, Ottawa. Ontario, Canada; and Solana Beach Presbyterian Church.

And now my ministry has been broadened even further, thanks to the encouragement to share my testimony from Paul Plew, The Master's College; Gordon Kirk, Lake Avenue Church; Janet Harms, Azusa Pacific University; Paul Brown, Shepherd's Community Church;

Lawrence Wilkes and Luis Lemos, The Crystal Cathedral; Roger Dermody, Bel Air Presbyterian Church; Bruce Rhodes, Miramonte School; Carlos Fernandez, Vanguard University; Pamela Leestma, Valley Christian Elementary School; Douglas Lawrence, Menlo Park Presbyterian Church; and Thomas Matrone, Central Assembly of God, Springfield, Missouri.

I want to especially thank Stephanie Edwards and Gary DeVaul for their participation in this benefit concert. And to Cathy and David Leestma and Bryan Jeffrey Leech for their assistance with the script. Thanks to Jan Rodger for editing Gary's new book, *Champions*. And sincere appreciation to Rick Dees for his radio program's financial assistance and to Randy Alley with Hanger Prosthetics for designing and developing my two new arms and three hands! To Julian Revie, who helped me proof my new organ book, *Organ Hymns of Faith, Volume 3* [the foreword and introduction to this are printed on the following pages], and to Jan Sanborn for her editorial assistance, I am grateful. Also, thanks to the Fred Bock Music Company for staffing the music table, and to Marilyn Gabriel and Amy Tan for coordinating the sale of compact discs.

To the Trust Fund Committee (Paul Bandy, chair) and the Concert Committee (Darlene and David Feit-Pretzer, co-chairs)...well done! And to John West for serving as the Trust Fund Committee's liaison for this evening's program, and also coordinating the September 10 Keyboard Benefit Concert with Christopher Pardini at The Crystal Cathedral, I am most appreciative.

Thank you ALL for the privilege of being a part of your lives! Thank you for your faithful prayers and continued care and kindness. God loves you and so do I!

Sincerely in Christ's service,

Mark A. Thallander

Organ Hymns of Faith
Volume 3
Foreword

I have great admiration and respect for the abilities of Mark Thallander. He was my long-time associate at the Crystal Cathedral, where he excelled in both administration and in service playing. His approach to the latter was always fitting and often quite stirring.

In this new collection of hymn arrangements he brings his hallmark sense of beauty and excitement coupled with his harmonic language and colorful expression linked to each hymn text.

Mark is not only gifted, he has incredible spirit. When this book is issued to coincide with a service and concert in his honor on March 21, 2004, it will remind us that less than eight months before Mark lost his left arm in a horrific car accident. His strong faith, super-positive outlook on life and amazing resourcefulness have him up, active, and making an incredible new life for himself. He is playing the organ again, and composed two of the arrangements in this collection to go with those written earlier.

I treasure Mark's friendship of many years, and find enormous inspiration in what he has done and in what he is accomplishing despite physical challenges that would overwhelm most people.

As you and your listeners enjoy playing and hearing the arrangements, give thanks that God not only spared Mark's life, but obviously still has great plans for him as he serves God in ministering to others.

Frederick Swann
National President, American Guild of Organists
Organist Emeritus, The Crystal Cathedral
Organist Emeritus, First Congregational Church of Los Angeles

Organ Hymns of Faith
Volume 3
Introduction

"Take my hands and let them move at the impulse of thy love; take my feet and let them be swift and beautiful for thee."

The words of this hymn had become my weekly prayer before starting the organ prelude. However, on January 25, 2004, my first time to play a complete Sunday morning service since my accident of August 3, 2003, I prayed differently. "Take my hand…" I then asked Jesus to be present – to be my strength – that the organ music would sound complete – and that in some awesome spiritual sense, Jesus would be my left hand.

I began with Fred Bock's majestic setting of *Old Hundredth*. And then that "historic" service at Bel Air Presbyterian Church continued. John West, artist-in-residence, had carefully crafted the worship to ensure my success. The choir was praying for me.

During the greeting time, a woman said to me, "I had no idea your arm had been amputated until the pastor mentioned it in the middle of the service."

My prayer had been answered. Jesus had come along side me. I was not alone in that service. And you are not alone, either. Jesus will never leave us or forsake us!

May these arrangements serve to assist you and your congregation in offering praise and worship to our loving and faithful God!

Mark Thallander

Mark autographs his new organ book, Organ Hymns of Faith, Volume 3.

Cantus Laudendi – Canticles of Praise
February 27, 2005
Lake Avenue Church
Pasadena, California

A MESSAGE
From Mark Thallander
President, The Mark Thallander Foundation

Dear Friends,

Welcome to *Cantus Laudendi – Canticles of Praise.* This is the first of many choral and organ festivals that will be presented by the new Mark Thallander Foundation. It is appropriate, then, that we joyfully celebrate God's faithfulness to us with great hymns of glorious praise. *"For you have been my help, and in the shadow of your wings I will sing for joy. My soul clings to you; your right hand upholds me."* (Psalm 63:7, 8)

One year ago, eight hundred voices joined together in an *Affirmation of Faith and Life.* The theme was from Proverbs 3:5, 6 – *"Trust in*

the Lord with all your heart, and lean not on your own understanding.
In all your ways acknowledge him, and he shall direct your paths."
This evening, those verses continue to be a part of our gathering
in Frederick Swann's anthem *Be Strong and Of Good Courage*. By
trusting in God, I have found a plan for my life. Certainly there
is growth during success, but a different kind of growth occurs
during trials. Trials are times when God sharpens us. We are able to
rejoice in tribulation – tribulation works endurance and endurance
hope. *"Let us then approach the throne of grace with confidence, so*
that we may receive mercy and find grace to help in our time of need."
(Hebrews 4:16)

In Isaiah 14:10, we find these words of hope: *"Fear not, I am with*
you; be not dismayed, for I am your God; I will strengthen you, I will
help you." And in Isaiah 41:13, *"For I, the Lord your God, hold your*
right hand; it is I who say to you, 'Fear not, I am the one who helps
you.'"

After the benefit program last March, a concert committee was
formed. We were inspired to begin dreaming about a vision and
a mission. A board of directors was established, and now a nonprofit organization has been birthed!

The past year has been an adventure with God. Before August 3,
2003, I was in the driver's seat; God was in the passenger's seat.
Now God is in the driver's seat. God takes me where I should go!
I have experienced God's right hand holding my right hand, and
I do believe that all things really do work together for good! This
evening, we launch a new Foundation with *Cantus Laudendi –*
Canticles of Praise. Its music is an extension of my heart of praise
to God for all that has been accomplished.

Thank you for your generous support of the Mark Thallander Trust
Fund this past year. The Trust Fund has blessed me and continues
to sustain me in significant ways. Thank you for your continued

love, care and kindness. Thank you for supporting our new dreams with your prayers and financial gifts. And thank you for allowing us to serve you a rich banquet of soul-nourishing and spirit-inspiring choral and organ music!

It is truly a triumph, in a society that often casts aside the traditional in favor of the immediate, to see hundreds of people of all ages, varied cultural backgrounds, and many faith traditions coming together in *"wonder, love and praise."*

May we all be ignited this evening to make God-like music in our lives! In the words of Isaac Watts,
"Love, so amazing, so divine, demands my soul, my life, my all!"

Mark Thallander

Note to Readers

To view Mark's calendar of coming events or to send Mark your greetings, log on to www.markthallander.com.

• •

If you would like to be an angel supporting Mark's continued recovery and ministry, you may send donations to:

The Mark A. Thallander Trust
P.O. Box 1614
Glendale, CA   91209-1614

Please make checks payable to the Mark A. Thallander Trust. Written correspondence may also be sent to this address. Thank you!

• •

Additional copies of this book may be ordered by writing to the Mark A. Thallander Trust at the address above. Ordering details are posted at www.markthallander.com. Mark's organ and piano CDs are also available through the Trust. Mark's published organ and choral music may be ordered from the Fred Bock Music Company (www.fredbock.com).

• •

For information on the music, mission, ministry, and upcoming events of the Mark Thallander Foundation or to secure recordings of Foundation Festivals, please log on to www. markthallanderfoundation.org.

Printed in the United States
200086BV00001B/1-129/A

9 781593 305017